Phillip Schofield's
One in a Million

PETER HOUGH

Michael O'Mara Books Limited

First published in 1996 by Michael O'Mara Books Limited
in association with London Weekend Television

Michael O'Mara Books Limited
9 Lion Yard, Tremadoc Road, London SW4 7NQ

A CIP catalogue number for this book is available from
the British Library

ISBN 1-85479-240-7

Designed and typeset by
K DESIGN, Winscombe, Somerset, England
Printed and bound in Great Britain by
Clays Ltd, St Ives plc

CONTENTS

ILLUSTRATIONS

John Wilkes Booth shoots President Lincoln (Hulton Getty)

President Kennedy with Evelyn Lincoln (Kennedy Library, Boston)

King Umberto I of Italy (Hulton Getty)

James Dean in a scene from *Giant* (National Film Archive)

Fate cover (Fortean Picture Library)

Fish dropping from the sky, 1555 (Fortean Picture Library)

Fish which fell on London in 1984 (Fortean Picture Library)

Montage of newspaper reports

Anthony Hopkins in the 1970s (Hulton Getty)

Poster for the film *The Girl from Petrovka* (Flashbacks)

The home of Camille Flammarion (Hulton Getty)

Conductor André Previn (Hulton Getty)

Camille Flammarion (Hulton Getty)

Main street in Lübeck (Hulton Getty)

Sketch map of the Bermuda Triangle (Syndication International)

Avenger torpedo bombers (Syndication International)

Welcome to the incredible world of coincidences and amazing one-in-a-million events.

Coincidences are one of my favourite subjects. Unlike other areas of strange experience, such as seeing ghosts or sighting the Loch Ness monster, with coincidences there is nothing to prove. Coincidences are so accessible. Almost everyone has a tale to tell about themselves, their family or their friends. Let me tell you about mine.

While I was working with the BBC Radio One *Roadshow*, we visited Newquay. It was a very special show for me because I had lived there many years before and vividly recalled sitting in the blistering hot sun and watching the *Roadshow* as an eleven-year-old budding DJ.

This time the organisers took me backstage to meet the policeman who would be looking after me. I couldn't work out why everyone was so amused – until I asked his name. It was PC Philip Schofield! A complete coincidence. . . .

I thought that was remarkable at the time, but it's nothing compared to the incredible stories told in the television series and in this book. Most people go an entire lifetime without witnessing a special one-in-a-million event. But in our studio and in the following pages we've got the largest collection of one-in-a-million stories ever assembled in one place.

It's difficult to explain why these things happen but, with 6 billion of us living on this planet, it's a certainty that something extraordinary is happening to someone somewhere at any given moment. We've found some amazing examples. Next time we could be telling the world about *you*.

Phillip Schofield

WHAT IS COINCIDENCE?

WHAT lies behind those one-in-a-million events that buck the trend, defy logic and throw cold water in the face of statistics? *Collins English Dictionary* defines coincidence as 'a chance occurrence of events remarkable for either being simultaneous or for apparently being connected'. If coincidences are the product of random chance events, why do certain of them have all the appearance of being 'engineered'? Is this possible and, if so, why?

There are roughly three categories of coincidence. Those that do appear to have a basis in the law of probability, coincidences that hint at some unknown power at work in the universe, and those with an element of precognition.

The phenomenon has long held a fascination for people. Mathematicians indulge themselves in working out the enormous odds of coincidences, and personal anecdotes provide entertainment in the pub or around the dinner table. One man took them very seriously: Swiss psychiatrist Carl Gustav Jung. In 1950 he coined a new term to describe 'meaningful' coincidences: synchronicity.

There are few people who have not experienced a 'meaningful coincidence'. Some coincidences are statistically insignificant chance groupings, but Jung realised that coincidences often had meaning to those directly involved. This seemed to be more than an illusion brought about by mere fortuity. Jung found it too incredible to accept 'chance' as the explanation in such cases.

He cited the case of a young woman who had come to him for psychoanalysis. At one point her progress faltered; then she had a dream of being given a golden scarab – a type of beetle which the ancient Egytians held as a potent symbol of regeneration. Jung wrote: 'While she was telling me this dream I sat with my back to the closed window. Suddenly, I heard a noise behind me, like a gentle tapping. I turned round and saw a flying insect knocking against the window pane from outside. I opened the window and caught the creature in the air as it flew in.'

Jung found that he held in his hand 'the nearest analogy to a golden scarab one finds in our latitudes, a scarabaeid beetle, the common rose-chafer, that contrary to its usual habits had evidently felt an urge to get into a dark room at this particular moment.'

The timely appearance of the scarab reinforced the effect the dream was already having on the woman, and the psychological barrier was overcome. Despite having been to two previous doctors, she was now able to continue her analysis and begin her transformation.

Jung speculated that synchronicity was brought about by the unconscious mind influencing external events in order to reinforce a point or convey information to the percipient. The following is a good illustration.

In 1943 Mr S. Messenger's older brother was reported missing, believed dead. He was just eighteen and had been stationed on a minesweeper for ten months. The family were never made aware of the full details of his death.

In February 1996 Messenger was browsing in his local library when he came across a book by Michael J. Melvin called *Minesweeper*. Curious to discover the kind of life his brother had led, he took it from the library to study. When Mr Messenger started reading the book, he discovered that it contained the full details of the tragedy which hit his brother's ship and even found his name listed. Messenger discovered the book on 21 February, which would have been his brother's seventieth birthday.

Synchronicity could also be an example of a universal principle at work – natural forces that endeavour to bring order out of chaos. Much of the time, however, there seems to be little purpose in coincidences other than to poke fun.

A set of coincidences involved the author of this book. They revolved around a photograph he was investigating purporting to show an alien. It was part of the evidence provided by a former police officer who had apparently been abducted on Ilkley Moor in December 1987. The photograph was under-exposed and blurred, leaving something to the imagination.

When the *Star* newspaper published the picture in July 1988, they claimed, tongue in cheek, to have solved the mystery. They said it showed an insurance salesman carrying a briefcase. The case was photographed, in a reconstruction, on the *right*-hand side of Jack McHale, who worked for the Prudential.

In February 1990 the *British Journal of Photography* published the results of computer image enhancement of the picture. The analyst, Geoffrey Crawley, had no knowledge of the newspaper scam two years earlier. Yet he too 'saw' a briefcase in the picture, but on the *left-hand side* of the figure.

At this time Peter Hough was working on a book called *Looking For The Aliens*, which included a serious discussion of the Ilkley photograph, making no reference to the bogus briefcase. A few months before publication in February 1992, the publisher sent Hough the proof of the book cover. It showed the silhouette of a humanoid figure. On the right-hand side was a briefcase. By the time of publication the briefcase had disappeared from the drawing.

The coincidences here seemed to be saying that the photograph should not, or could not, be taken seriously. Forteans – the generic name for followers of Charles Fort, an American who collated hundreds of mysteries – blame the 'Cosmic Joker' when confronted with absurd and humorous coincidences, as if there is some force loose in the universe making fun of us.

Jung also developed the idea of the 'collective unconscious'. He postulated that there exists a super mind which binds all of us together. It contains every thought every one of us has ever had. Individuals can – by accident or design – plug into this mind and the result is a psychic experience.

In 1981 former Cambridge University research fellow Dr Rupert Sheldrake took this idea a stage further. He called it the 'morphic resonance' theory and suggested that all living creatures are bound together by a 'morphic field'. This allows them to share and benefit from the experiences of others – past and present. It could unconsciously 'guide' people to make certain choices, which would then be interpreted as 'coincidence'.

Robert Matthews, a visiting research fellow at Aston University who specialises in the effects of probability theory, cites a recent example as a possible demonstration of Sheldrake's theory.

For over 250 years practitioners of bell-ringing have unsuccessfully attempted to carry out a complicated routine called the 'common bob Stedman triples'. On 22 January 1995 a team at St John's Church, London, finally succeeded. Almost at once it emerged that two other independent groups of bell-ringers had also solved the centuries old mystery. Synchronicity or simply the results of probability?

Coincidences are not the only 'one-in-a-million' incidents that concern us in this book. What about people who defy death against all the odds or pets that find their way home across miles of open countryside, crossing rivers and motorways? Then there are strange things which apparently fall from the sky – ice blocks, fish, frogs, and even golf balls!

Statistics show that someone somewhere is about to become embroiled in a one-in-a-million event. Be prepared. . . .

— · 1 · —

LOST AND FOUND

Some of the most amazing coincidences concern the discovery of personal items lost in circumstances where the owners never expect to see them again.

TWIST IN THE TALE

CAMILLE Flammarion, author of *The Unknown*, published in 1902, reveals a curious experience he had while working on a book about the atmosphere. He had completed a chapter on the wind when a gust carried the papers off 'in a miniature whirlwind beyond hope of recovery' out through the window of his study. Several days later he received the proofs of the missing chapter from his printer, Lahure, together with the original papers. Astounded, he contacted the firm and learned what had happened.

Apparently the papers had been deposited in a nearby street frequented by a porter who worked for the printer. Recognising the author's name, he thought he had dropped them on a previous errand when he had collected some of Flammarion's other chapters for proof setting, and took them to work with him.

A similar situation arose in London early in 1992, only on this occasion the author thought his manuscript had been rejected! Carmen Callil, then head of the London publishing firm Chatto & Windus, was dining out one Friday evening when her car was broken into. Amongst the items stolen was a manuscript for which she had high hopes. Ms Callil had not yet told the author, and now she was presented with the problem of telling him that his book had been stolen.

On the Monday morning she resolved to contact him but, before she could do so, a call came through to her office from the author. He was upset and asked her: 'Why did you have my manuscript thrown over my front fence?'

Despite the vagaries of the business, he was not used to publishers treating his work in this way. Apparently, the thieves, seeing no value in the typewritten pages, had hurled the manuscript out through the window of their car.

Actor Anthony Hopkins agreed to play a leading role in the 1974 film of the novel *The Girl From Petrovka* by George Feiffer. His attempts at acquiring a copy of the book to give him an insight into the story were not successful. After trawling the London bookshops he went to catch a tube train at Leicester Square and noticed a book discarded on a platform seat. It was a copy of the novel he had been searching for. Someone had scribbled notes in the margin, but he was pleased to have found it at last.

When Hopkins finally went abroad to start filming, he met George Feiffer for the first time. The author complained that he had lost his own copy of the novel which he had annotated. Apparently, a friend had borrowed it and mislaid it in London. The actor produced the copy he had found at Leicester Square. It was Feiffer's lost book.

Just as amazing is the experience of musician and conductor

André Previn. During a tour of Germany in 1985 he went for a walk with colleague Gil Shaham through the medieval town of Lübeck. As they passed an antiquarian bookseller's shop Previn noticed some books in the window with old German lettering. He told his friend that his father once had a library full of books like that. Later, Shaham suggested he go back and buy one.

At first they could not find the shop, but just as Previn was about to give up, they came across it again. He went in and bought two volumes by Thomas Mann, *The Magic Mountain* and *Buddenbrooks*.

That night, in his Hamburg hotel room, Previn undid the small parcel to examine his purchase. The musician was astounded to discover that one of the books had belonged to his father! It had his name in it. Previn's father had never been in Lübeck; indeed the musician was not supposed to be there either. The family had emigrated from Berlin to America in 1938.

Books seem to have a habit of coming home. Mrs S.C.M. Hill from London told the *Sunday Express* in July 1980 how her mother bought some children's books at a jumble sale, intending to read them to a young relative who was coming to stay. When she examined one of the books more closely, she discovered Mrs Hill's name and address on the fly leaf, written by her twenty-five years earlier, when she was only five. There was also a half-written letter Mrs Hill had penned to an aunt still between the pages.

Mrs E. Owens of Bristol described how her brother, who had emigrated to Canada, wrote and asked if a book he had owned as a child was still around. But it had apparently gone to a jumble sale years earlier. A week later in a second-hand bookshop Mrs Owens spotted a copy of the book and decided to buy it for her brother. When she opened it to see the price, she found her brother's name written inside.

THE FRENCH CONNECTION

AUTHOR Ken Anderson was told the following by leading Australian astrologer Stella Recamier. On her son Roger's eighth birthday in 1976 she sent him out on an errand in the Sydney suburb where they lived. As he set off she was reminded of her own eighth birthday.

On that day she was living in France and was travelling to Nice by bus with her parents. Along the way they had stopped at Avignon and in a shop Stella had noticed a small brass-framed mirror with a picture of the town on the back. She had wanted to buy it, but her parents had hurried her away as a bus was due.

Her reverie of her childhood was broken by the realisation that Roger had been gone a long time. When he did appear, the boy had no idea of the impact his excuse was to have on his mother. He told her that on his way home he had been attracted by a roadside stall selling bric-a-brac, and had decided to buy his mother a gift. Roger held the gift out to her – it was the same brass-framed mirror she had wanted all those years ago complete with a picture of Avignon on the back. Stella had never told her son the story, and it was only Roger's eighth birthday that had made Stella recall her own.

LOST AND FOUND, AND LOST AGAIN

THE mysterious disappearance of 'Flight 19' in the so-called Bermuda Triangle received a boost in May 1991. The mystery began when five Avenger torpedo bombers took off from a US Navy base at Fort Lauderdale for target practice off the coast of Bimini on 5 December 1945. After the first run they regrouped, but then inexplicably failed to recognise their surroundings. Lt Charles Taylor radioed the base, saying: 'We seem to be lost... Everything is wrong, strange... We can't be sure of any direction... even the ocean doesn't look as it should.' Confused scraps of conversation between the crew broken up by static hinted at malfunctioning compasses, high winds and low fuel.

Despite a massive search the following day by an armada of nearly 100 ships and several submarines, no wreckage or bodies were ever found. Critics of the mystery pointed out that the crew were inexperienced and a sudden storm might have thrown them off course until they eventually ditched after running out of fuel. However, at the time of the disappearance records showed the weather was near perfect.

It appeared that the critics were about to be proved right when, on 17 May 1991, it was announced that Flight 19 had been found – on the bottom of the ocean bed. A salvage team looking for treasure off the coast of Florida had discovered the wreckage of five Avengers. The number '28' was on one of them – the same as one of the lost planes.

Two weeks later the news was rescinded. It turned out that the aircraft were *not* from the lost squadron. The Avengers were an earlier model and were the remains of a floating target range which was sunk between 1943 and 1945. So Flight 19 was lost, found and then lost again....

DAGGERS

BERT Clark served in the RAF between 1941 and 1946. On VJ Day 1945 he was in an Austrian village called

Frohnleiten, near Graz in Austria. His unit had taken over a *schloss* and they stayed there for nine months. During this time he collected wartime memorabilia, and a young lad used to bring him souvenirs in exchange for chocolate. Bert never enquired where these artefacts had come from, one of which was a German ceremonial dagger.

In 1995, during the VE celebrations, he wrote to the Mayor of Frohnleiten to ask if anyone remembered his unit being there, as Bert had fond memories of the place. After a while he received a reply from a Fritz Maier who, although born in Frohnleiten, had moved to Hastings in 1994. As Bert's daughter lived in nearby Rye, he arranged to meet Fritz during a visit to her.

Bert took photographs and a copy of a book he had written about his wartime experiences to show Fritz. When Fritz came across a picture of the dagger, he became very excited and asked where Bert had obtained it. It transpired that it was Fritz's father's dagger that had been buried at the end of the war.

BURIED AND FOUND

ERIC Lawes, a retired gardener, found more than a dagger when he went looking for lost tools in a farmer's field. In November 1992 he took his metal detector to the field in Hoxne, Suffolk, and found several old coins close to the surface. Acting on a strong signal from the detector, he dug deeper and unearthed two bags full of Roman coins. Later a total of 14,780 items were recovered including gold jewellery, silver spoons, ladles, bowls and figures made from silver.

It became known as the 'Hoxne Hoard' – the finest collection of Roman treasures found in Britain. In September 1995 the authorities decided that the items had been buried with the intention of recovery, as opposed to being 'lost'. This meant that they were regarded as treasure trove, and subsequently the collection was sold for £1.75 million, which was divided between sixty-year-old Mr Lawes and the farmer who owned the land, Peter Watling.

LOST DOWN THE LOO

BARBARA Hutton was upset when she accidentally flushed her antique bracelet down the toilet with a bundle of tissues. Seventeen months later, Barbara, a secretary who lives in Woodley, Berkshire, went into a shop to buy a piece of jewellery. While she was there, a man walked in and ask for a valuation on a bracelet. Barbara immediately recognised it as the one she had lost and blurted out her story to the man. He admitted to having found it while working in a sewer six months before and handed it back to her. She told reporters in November 1975: 'The man couldn't have known the bracelet belonged to me. It was amazing. That he should be in the same shop on the same day is just fantastic.'

A RING TO IT

THERE are many stories connected with rings lost and found. Joseph Cross lost his ring in 1980 while boating across Hampton Roads near Houston, Texas. It was knocked from his hand during a storm and sank into the channel waters.

In February 1982 it was found in a fish destined for a restaurant in Charlottesville. Mr Cross was traced through an inscription.

Tony Wells was not very pleased when his wife told him she had lost her wedding ring while they were on holiday at Barmouth, west Wales. They never expected to see it again. Three weeks later the couple returned to Barmouth from their home in Stourport to collect sea shells and found the ring.

It was on St Anne's beach in Lancashire that Brenda Rawson lost her diamond engagement ring. She and her fiancé, Christopher Firth, visited the beach on six successive weekends to sift the sand, but it seemed lost forever. The following year they married and continued to check with St Anne's police station when they returned for holidays in case someone had handed the ring in.

In 1977, sixteen years after the ring had been lost, Christopher's uncle died and he discovered the whereabouts of a long lost cousin. John lived not far away from Brenda and Christopher in Yorkshire. On one of their visits, which took place in July 1979, the conversation turned to metal detectors. John told Brenda that one of his children had found a diamond ring on St Anne's beach eighteen years before. It was her engagement ring. . . .

Thekla Aanen of Larkollen in Norway was swimming in an Oslo fiord in 1976 when she lost her diamond ring. Three years later Robert, her grandson, was fishing in the fiord when he caught a ten-pound salmon. In triumph he brought it home for his grandmother, and Thekla gutted it for supper. She was amazed to find her ring inside it.

Fish are not the only places where lost rings have turned up. Here is a story about one which was found in a pile of manure!

It began in 1943, when Ken Peel started courting a girl called Marion. They became engaged in 1945 and finally married a year later on 9 February at St Lawrence's Church in Tingley near Sheffield. At the time Kenneth was in the RAF and had to get special leave.

Although the couple did not have much money, they took great care in selecting their wedding ring. It was just a plain circle of nine-carat gold, but it meant a great deal to them. Mrs Peel explained: 'There wasn't a lot of choice in those days. Wedding rings were very hard to come by. A lot of people got them handed down from parents and grandparents. Ours was a new one, which we were very proud of.' Despite rationing, it was quite a big wedding. Everyone baked and cooked something for the reception.

The coupled moved into a cottage not far from Broadhurst Farm. While Mr Peel was abroad with the RAF, his wife took to helping out on the farm. She enjoyed being with the animals, milking, and cleaning out the poultry and pigs. Ken also lent a hand while on leave and sometimes felt he was better suited to farming than engineering. Then one day, while he was away, Marion wrote him a letter in which she told him of the loss of the precious wedding ring.

It happened at the farm when one of the cows gave birth to a bull calf. The animal was taken away from its mother and put in a small pen. Marion thought she would give the calf a drink, so she went and found a bucket, which she filled with milk from the dairy. She tried to console the calf, which was distressed at being parted from its mother, and let it suckle milk off her fingers. When the calf had finished, she gave it a stroke and picked up the bucket. It was then that she noticed her wedding ring was missing.

'I felt so stunned,' she said, 'I just couldn't believe it. The calf had taken my wedding ring!'

She went and told some men who worked on the farm what

had happened. They just laughed at first, which made her more upset. They agreed to keep an eye out for the ring in the manure, although there was not much hope of ever seeing it again. The manure in the shed was already a foot deep. As each layer formed, it was mixed in with straw. There were seven other calves born at that time too, adding to the complications, so it was really an impossible task. Ken wrote back to Marion and told her not to worry, but he was quite upset at the time. She ended up wearing her grandmother's ring until she could afford another.

Some months later a mountain of manure was brought from the farm and left at the back of the Peels' cottage ready to be spread over the fields. Ken decided to use some of it on his vegetable patch. He was forking it into a wheelbarrow when he noticed something stuck on one of the tines.

'I cleared the dirt away and saw it was a ring. After carefully removing it from the tine, I carried it to the water tank and washed it. Then I could see it was my wife's wedding ring!'

Marion was in the kitchen when Ken appeared and asked her to hold out her hand. 'I automatically held out my right hand, but he said, "No, the other one." He had his fist curled up and I wondered if it was a practical joke. When he dropped the ring into my palm, it was unbelievable!'

Marion had to sit down. Off came grandma's ring and on went her own. It was like getting married all over again.

MONEY, MONEY, MONEY

Doyle Love of Portland, Oregon, thought he would never see his wallet again when he went fishing in August 1977. It fell into the Pacific Ocean while he was casting a line. However, on Sunday 21 August, a gill-netter from Naselle, Washington named Ralph Mossitt caught the wallet in his net near the mouth of the Columbia River. He posted it back to Love, who figured the odds of finding it were 'one in ten million'.

When Ellen Rice of Borger, Texas sent her great-grandson a one-dollar bill in February 1984, naturally she never expected to see it again. The bill was inscribed with the boy's name – 'James Hoil Green' – and he went and spent it in Oklahoma City. In June the same bill was tendered at a concession stand in Texas – run by Mrs Rice.

It looks as if it is not only bad pennies that have a habit of turning up. Mrs M. Coyle of Glasgow told the *Sun* on 19 August 1971: 'For years I carried in my purse a lucky sixpence with my initials on it. The day before I went to Ireland on holiday, I accidentally spent it. Two days later, in a small Irish village, I had the sixpence back in change.'

A bank note with a cryptic message on it seemed to exert a strange influence on Mrs Kathleen Jackson, according to a report in the *Sunday Express* for 22 August 1982. The pound note was given her in change while shopping in her home town of Huntington, north Yorkshire. On it was written: '9 for bank 1 Andrew'. The following day Mrs Jackson and her family drove to a caravan site near Kirkcudbright, Scotland, for a holiday. As she used the note to pay for food, a strange feeling washed over her – *she felt a strong compulsion to keep it, but did not in fact do so*.

Five days later, when she was back home, she went out shopping again. Mrs Jackson was dumbstruck when a shopkeeper handed her the pound note in her change. There was no doubt it was the same one – it had the same message on it in the same handwriting, in exactly the same position on the note. The serial number AX27 743180 was one of 657 million notes in circulation at that time.

NOT LOST – BUT FOUND

MRS Slack of Oxford remembers the time when her husband, Peter, decided to change his old record player for something more up to date. His friend John was also in the market for something new, and they discussed the pros and cons for weeks.

Eventually John ordered a lot of sophisticated equipment, while Peter bought a music centre, which arrived in its original packaging from the factory. A certain amount of assembling had to be done by Peter, but this was no problem and the music centre worked perfectly – but there was one bit left over.

In the meantime John changed his mind and cancelled his order, buying a music centre instead – the same make as Peter's, but a different model. However, when it was assembled, John could not get it to work because there was a bit missing. It turned out to be the extra piece that Peter had found in his packaging!

SOME WELLY

WHEN Sarah Clay went on a school trip to an outward bound centre, she took with her a good pair of Wellington boots. It was the middle of winter with a few inches of snow on the ground. Decked out in a wet suit and boiler suit, she joined other students in exploring a pothole. They were underground for about four hours in the extreme cold.

'The cave was flooded and we were told to drop down into a stream and let it carry us back to the entrance. I started to swim and felt my boot come off under the water. The current was strong and the stream deep so there was no hope of finding it.'

Sarah was so cold she really didn't care. Finally she scrambled up some rocks to the cave extrance, where she joined the rest of the group.

Outside she tripped over a lump in the snow. Her teacher asked how she was going to walk back with only one boot, but Sarah was busy uncovering the buried object. She could not believe it. She had found another Wellington boot... Sarah answered her teacher with: 'It's all right, I've found one here!' It was the right foot and exactly the right size, but a different shape and colour.

Sarah said: 'I can't usually get shoes because I'm a size eight, and that's fairly big for a girl. It was only the first day of the trip, so I don't know what I would have done without it. To have found a boot at all would have been odd enough after just losing one, but the facts that no one had noticed it on the way into the cave, and that it was the right foot and size seem really bizarre.'

TWO FINGERS

THIS has to be one of the strangest 'lost and found' stories ever written. The London *Evening Standard* reported in its edition of 24 May 1996 that a man had been reunited with his two missing fingers after twenty-five years! The fingers were found by demolition workers in Sydney, Australia, in a pile of wallpaper. One had a nicely manicured nail, and both were very well preserved.

Initially police thought they were dealing with a murder and cordoned off the house while they looked for further evidence of a dismembered body. Then they thought the fingers had been taken from an embalmed corpse and had them rehydrated so that fingerprints could be taken. Finally a fifty-nine-year-old man came forward who lived in the house between 1968 and 1988. He said the fingers were his. They had been cut off twenty-five years before in an accident with a circular saw.

FOUND – AT LAST

WASHING-MACHINE engineer Les Horan spent thirty years searching for the grave of his father killed in World War II. Horan's father had been in the Royal New Zealand Air Force. His Sea Otter plane had been shot down by Japanese fighters on 9 January 1945 off the coast of the island of Akyab near Burma.

One summer's day in 1995 Horan was called out to a job in a flat at Bromsgrove, Worcestershire. Noticing an RAF plaque in the hall, he told the owner, Joe Grainger, about his world-wide search for his father's grave, commenting that 'no one seems to have heard of Akyab'.

Surprisingly, Grainger *had* heard of Akyab; in fact he had been there. The wartime veteran told the engineer that his unit had taken part in the 1945 invasion of Akyab, but could not remember any casualties. Then he recalled that on the day after the invasion, 9 January, he had gone for a swim and found an airman's body washed up on the beach. This was identified as John Horan and buried in the civil cemetery with Grainger in charge of the bearers. Later it was reinterred in the military cemetery in Rangoon.

After three decades of searching as far afield as New Zealand, just two miles from his home Les Horan had discovered the whereabouts of his father's final resting place.

MISSING TIME

ALEXANDRA Martin from Aldershot recounted a story involving her cousin Jessica. Jessica's godmother gave her a pretty gold wristwatch for her birthday, which the girl admired constantly. One night Jessica and Alexandra went to the cinema. Afterwards Jessica and her boyfriend disappeared around the back of the building on to some waste land, while Alexandra waited for them at a nearby fish and chip shop.

When they were late turning up, she went in search of the couple and found them on their knees among the weeds looking for Jessica's watch. Alexandra suggested they return the following morning in daylight, which they did, but there was no sign of the watch, nor had it been handed in at the cinema or the local police station.

Five years later Jessica was at the cinema again, which by now had been converted to a bingo hall. She was engaged to a different young man, who she had arranged to meet at the end of the night. They disappeared to the same patch of land where she had previously lost her watch.

Jessica stumbled over a Cadbury's Roses box, picked it up to make sure it was empty and found her watch inside. There was no doubt it was the same watch. How had it got there? Why had five years of wet and damp weather done it no harm? Jessica wound it up and it kept perfect time.

Watches lost in rivers, like rings, often have a curious way of being returned to their owners. A Ukrainian woman was helping her husband, Alexander Taran, set up his angling equipment beside the River Dnieper in the summer of 1979 when she unwittingly dropped her gold wristwatch in the water. Several days later Mr Taran returned to the spot to do some more fishing and reeled in a seven-pound pike. When his wife gutted it, she found her watch inside its belly.

A Texas cattle farmer called Paul Watson also dropped his gold watch in a river whilst fishing. Three days later his thirteen-year-old son, Jack, went fishing at the same spot with some friends. Jack caught the only fish of the day and the boys prepared to cook it over an open fire. They gutted the fish and there was Paul's father's watch.

MESSAGE IN A BOTTLE

THE story of the sailor washed ashore and marooned on a desert island sending for help by sealing a message in a bottle and casting it out to sea is not as far fetched as it seems. There are several cases on file where bottles have successfully journeyed thousands of miles.

Vicki Thomas was eight years old when she launched a Coca-Cola bottle containing a message from a beach in Bognor Regis. Many others have done this and the vast majority never expect nor receive a reply. For Vicki it was different. Three years later, the day before her eleventh birthday, she received a letter from twenty-nine-year-old Andrew Fitch all the way from Australia. Andrew explained how he had discovered the bottle on a beach in Geraldton, Western Australia. The pair have kept in touch with one another, and Andrew regularly sends Vicki presents.

As if such fantastic journeys are not enough, there are others with an extra twist. David Lawson Kerr from Scotland was on the Gambian coast when he decided to toss a message bottle into the sea. It travelled 3,000 miles and was washed ashore eight months later on Fowl Bay Beach, St Philip, Barbados. The beach was owned by another David Lawson.

When Mrs Lena McCovey's house on the Klamath river, USA, was destroyed by flood waters, along with other household items that were washed away was a bottle of prescription pills to calm her nerves. These turned up 200 miles away in Coos Bay, Oregon – discovered by Mrs McCovey's sister. Perhaps the forces behind such coincidences decided that Mrs McCovey needed her pills back to help her cope with the tragedy.

TEETH 'R' US

THE late Loch Ness Monster hunter Tim Dinsdale described how, many years ago, his uncle lost his false teeth whilst swimming at Borth, on the Welsh coast north of Aberystwyth. About three months later a relative trod on them whilst bathing, and they were put back to use.

Roy Peters of Bristol similarly went swimming at Beer in Devon. When he opened his mouth, his top set of teeth fell out and sank. Some years later he went back to the resort and learned that a set of dentures had been washed up on the beach in a storm and handed in to a local café. He tried them and found they were his.

RAISE YOUR GLASSES

IN July 1982, while fly-fishing on the Ystwyth river in Wales, Dr Peter Callaghan accidentally cast his spectacles into the water. A neighbour of his, Will Jones, of Llanilar, Dyfed, totally unaware of the doctor's accident, went fishing in the same river – and reeled in the missing glasses.

A story that also seems to involve a degree of ESP was related to the *Sunday Express* in November 1971 by Bill Lees. Mr Lees lost his spectacles when he dived into the sea off Benidorm in

Spain. It was only later that he realised he must have been wearing them at the time. During the night a feeling took hold of him that he knew *exactly* where they were. The following morning his daughter bought some diving goggles and the pair rowed out and found the glasses in fifteen feet of water.

PICTURE THIS

M R G. Ashworth from Oldham, Lancashire has a strange story to tell of when he went fishing in June or July 1945. At that time Mr Ashworth was aboard the HMS *Cosby*, anchored in Falmouth Bay. To supplement their 'dull rations' some of the men decided to fish for mackerel over the side of the ship. They had an arrangement with the chef. He would cook their catch if they cleaned the fish first. Mr Ashworth was gutting a mackerel when he found something he had not bargained for.

'I was somewhat surprised to discover inside the gullet a photograph! It was tightly rolled and perfectly preserved. A picture of an attractive lady with a message written in Italian on the back. The message, *Amore mio ti amo cosi tanto tua*, when translated, said – 'My Love, I love you so much. . .'

The story was published in the *Daily Express*, and several days later the photograph was claimed by a woman called Bianca Dault who managed the George Hotel in Largs, Strathclyde. She was Italian, and her husband, a French merchant seaman, had kept the photograph with him at sea. He had been serving on a ship in an Atlantic convoy when it was attacked by the Germans and he was lost at sea.

The picture was reunited with its original owner in circumstances which would have been impossible to foresee – or calculate the odds on.

– · 2 · –
FANTASTIC JOURNEYS

How can some animals, marooned miles from home, find their way back over terrain they are totally unfamiliar with? In December 1973 it was reported how Armin da Broi of Solingen in Germany sold Barry, a huge Alsatian, to his neighbour. The new owner took the dog with him to Bari in southern Italy, where it escaped. A year later Barry turned up on Armin's doorstep, having travelled at least 1,200 miles!

An unusual case involved a pregnant heifer which was sold by Sidney Krafsow of Seminole County in central Florida to rancher Read Hayes, who was based in neighbouring Orange County. Overnight the cow disappeared and returned to Mr Krafsow the following evening. Somehow the animal had travelled thirty-five miles, negotiating fences, rivers and highways.

There are many other accounts of such fantastic journeys, but not all are easy to verify. Here is one that *did* check out – the story of Bodie the dog.

THE LONG AND WINDING ROAD

VAL and Tony Finnan annually attended the Pickering steam fair in north Yorkshire from their home in Conisbrough, near Doncaster. They took their caravan and ran a stall selling fine art framed prints. In July 1995 they decided to take their labrador-Doberman cross, Bodie, with them. It was a decision they were to regret.

On the night of 29 July there was a firework display at the fair. At 10.20 pm exactly a banger exploded – and Bodie bolted. The Finnans searched until the early hours, but there was no sign of the dog. In the morning the couple ran their stall as usual, but their hearts were not in it. After the fair finished on the Sunday night, Val and Tony stayed on, hoping their pet would show, but to no avail. They were devastated. The dog had disappeared, but the couple were determined not to give up.

They made cardboard 'lost dog' signs, which they put up around the pubs and shops where the steam fair had been held. Val and Tony stopped people in the street and even involved a local newspaper in their search. Back in Conisbrough they began receiving two to three telephone calls a day from people who had sighted the animal, but no one had been able to catch him. Locals said they had seen him around Pickering, behaving like a wild dog. A month after Bodie had disappeared the calls dried up.

Tony took the caravan back up to Pickering and actually saw the dog twice. He tried tempting Bodie with chocolate, but he acted as if he did not recognise his owner and ran away. Val saw him once. Eventually, feeling very glum, they had no choice but to return home to Conisbrough without Bodie.

Seven and a half weeks after the firework had sent the dog off in a blind panic, the Finnans were at home watching television.

It was the evening of 20 September. They became aware of a scratching sound on their front door. Val opened the door and in walked Bodie ... He was thin, tired, sore, flea-ridden and smelly. He wagged his tail, barked and went to each of them in turn. They fed him some chocolate and he settled down as if he had never been away. Afterwards the Finnans were able to piece together Bodie's remarkable journey.

The dog had spent the first two weeks in the area where the steam fair had been held, scavenging. Then he moved to Pickering for the next fortnight, eating hotel scraps. After a month of this he had apparently decided to come home, and his incredible journey began.

Over the next few weeks, during his journey south, he was sighted in Malton, Fridaythorpe, Newton upon Derwent, Sutton upon Derwent, Melbourne, Foggathorpe, Stainforth and finally Conisbrough... How had this incredible feat been achieved? Bodie had travelled over eighty miles across land he had never set foot on before. There was no scent, no familiar landmarks. He had crossed the River Ouse, several railway lines, the A1, the M62 and M18.

Roger Mugford of the Animal Behaviour Centre believes that most animals are very sensitive to magnetic fields and can automatically guide themselves to a destination like someone following the needle of a compass. Once Bodie was close to home visual and olfactory senses would take over to pinpoint his exact route.

Bloodhounds have an exceptionally strong sense of smell, which probably accounts for this tale. Even so ...

Ever since Angus the bloodhound was a pup his owner, Mick Harrison, had worn a pair of burgundy slippers. Angus would bring the slippers to his master every evening and enjoyed the ritual. Then, on Christmas Day 1985, Mick's wife Susan bought him a new pair. The old slippers were taken with some other rubbish to the council tip about two miles from their home in Pudsey, Yorkshire. Angus accompanied Mick to the dump.

The following day, when Susan took Angus for a run in the fields near their house, Angus disappeared. Susan searched for a while and then went home. An hour or so later the dog returned – carrying Mick's old burgundy slippers in his mouth.

ARE CATS FAMILIAR WITH ESP?

CATS can become part of the family while remaining aloof and independent. They are very territorial. At times it seems they can read your mind and almost talk. Their very individualistic nature has ensured their place in mythology. The witch's cat is all too familiar.

Keele University has carried out research on cats which indicates that they too are sensitive to electromagnetic fields. The University of California has found that they are intuitively aware of seismic stress and can anticipate earthquakes, which they indicate by their behaviour. It would seem that animals possess a sixth sense which humans have lost.

There are many stories of cats finding their way home over large distances and under 'impossible' conditions. Is a sensitivity to electromagnetic fields evidence of extrasensory perception (ESP)?

In August 1973 Whisky the cat was given away to a family in Cambridge. Shortly afterwards he disappeared. Twenty-five days later he returned to his original owners in Bingley, Yorkshire, having covered 150 miles. Did he follow a scent, as some experts believe? How could he when no scent trail was left by his former owners, who travelled by motor car? Whisky did not find his way home through trial and error. He had travelled six miles a day and knew precisely in which direction to go. Did he, as was suggested with Bodie the dog, use his visual and olfactory senses to guide him the last short distance home?

When Smokey's family decided to move house he did not share their enthusiasm. En route he leapt from the car and vanished. Smokey – recognisable by a dark red tuft on his head – showed up two weeks later at the family's *new* home.

Some research into this amazing ability was carried out in the 1970s at the Institute of Parapsychology in Durham, North Carolina. They analysed and investigated many stories of cat journeys, then carried out some experiments to test for ESP.

In one of them two sealed containers were placed at either end of a room full of hungry cats. One container was empty, the other was filled with meat. The scientists went to great lengths to ensure that all smells were eliminated from the exterior of the containers and the room itself. Although the cats could not see the food, the majority went to the container of meat. Did they use ESP?

THE TORTOISE THAT WENT WALKABOUT
FOR THIRTY-FIVE YEARS!

MALCOLM Edwards was just eight when his pet tortoise, Chester, went missing in 1960. Nothing was seen of him until thirty-five years later in 1985, when cyclist Flossie Masshder found the mud-splattered creature at the side of the road in Lyde, Hereford.

She spotted a fading white mark on his shell and began

knocking on doors to find out who was the owner. When she showed it to Malcolm, he recognised it immediately. His father had painted on the mark over three decades earlier.

Vet George Cooper was sure it was Chester. He said the tortoise looked between forty-five and forty-six years of age, and could easily have survived in local woodland.

In Williamston, Michigan, Melvin Beach had his turtle returned to him *sixty* years after it was lost. The reptile was identified by Beach's initials, which were engraved upon its shell in 1919!

— ·3· —
NAMES AND NUMBERS

IT is amazing how the coincidence of names, words and numbers intrudes on our daily routine. One sometimes gains the impression that behind many events in our apparently random lives lurks a comedy scriptwriter quietly chuckling to himself as we shake our heads in wonder.

The *Weekly News* reported in May 1976 how an obstetrician named Don Triplet had recently delivered his third set of triplets. In that same year the Cosmic Joker was having some fun with the Royal Society for the Protection of Birds. It all came to light when Mr Allan Bird joined the RSPB's headquarters in Sandy, Bedfordshire, as an assistant reserve manager. Among his colleagues were, incredibly, Barbara Buzzard, John Partridge, Celia and Helen Peacock and Dorothy Rook. Peter Condor had recently retired as director.

Elsewhere PC David Bird investigated the theft of 10,800 eggs in Bristol. Inspector Derek Bird led a hunt for an ostrich near Bristol in March 1979, assisted by his boss, Chief Inspector Plume.

ACCIDENTAL NAMES

A car pile-up in Riom, France, on 3 August 1975 left the drivers with no problem remembering one another's names. A car driven by Jean-Pierre Serre of Paris crashed into a car driven by Georges Serre of Clermont-Ferrand. Just seconds later another car piled into the first two – driven by Mlle C. Serre of Royat. The drivers were not related and had never met before. Serre is not even a common name in France. Out of a listing of 1,200,000 entries in the Paris telephone directory there are only 120 Serres.

SECURITY IN MARRIAGE WITHOUT COLOUR PREJUDICE

MARRIAGE really means something in Australia. Barman Thomas Key married Ann Lock. Twenty years later their only child, Bill Key, married Ellen Bolt, daughter of Harry Bolt and the former Ms Evelyn Chain.

Over in Wakefield, Yorkshire, there was a colourful wedding in 1967. When Valerie Brown married Alan Black, their wedding was attended by eleven Blacks, eight Browns, five Whites, five Greens and four Greys!

NEVER A CROSS WORD

JUST prior to the Normandy landings on 6 June 1944, the *Daily Telegraph* published a crossword that made those in authority believe they had a spy in their midst. The puzzle contained many of the top secret code names used in the operation: Omaha, Mulberry, Utah, Neptune plus the name for D-day itself – Overlord. Military Intelligence officers interviewed the compiler – an innocent schoolmaster – and came away baffled.

A crossword puzzle also played a part in a more recent coincidence. Two elderly ladies, Margaret Lea and her friend 'Dorrie', went for a holiday on the Mediterranean island of Crete in 1995. They always go to the same place twice a year. Margaret and Dorrie were relaxing on the sea front doing the *Daily Telegraph* crossword puzzle when they were mulling over a clue. It said: 'The Chancellor of the Exchequer 1974–1979.' They both spoke out loud the answer and wrote down Denis Healey – just as he turned the corner and walked towards them! The former Labour chancellor cheerily called out, 'Good afternoon, ladies', and joined them for a chat with his wife. They explained the remarkable coincidence, and Denis Healey afterwards confirmed the story.

FREUDIAN SLIP?

NATURALIST Sir Peter Scott was a believer in the Loch Ness Monster. In the mid 1970s he produced an oil painting depicting the plesiosaur-like creatures, and a schoolteacher suggested a scientific name for the beast, *Nessiteras rhombopteryx*. This attempt to give the phenomenon greater credibility backfired when, on 13 December 1975, several national newspapers revealed that the new name was an anagram for 'Monster Hoax by Sir Peter S'.

THE WORD OF ALLAH

IN recent years designs created to adorn a variety of merchandise coincidentally resembled Islamic holy writing, thus upsetting members of Muslim communities. Thousands of shoes manufactured in China were seized in 1985 by the Egyptian authorities when it was found that the pattern of the anti-slip treads read as the Arabic for 'Allah' when the image was reversed.

In April 1992 a Nottingham fashion shop fell foul of Islam when it began selling high-quality Italian shoes deliberately adorned with the Arabic verse 'There is no God but Allah'. Haji Mohammed Asmat, vice chairman of the Nottingham Islamic Centre demanded that the owner withdraw the shoes from sale and apologise. The Italian-born owner of the shop, Mrs Diana Lewis, refused to withdraw the shoes, but reached a compromise with the Islamic community when a wealthy Muslim bought the last dozen pairs and then burnt them. This was not the end of the matter, however. A car was later driven through the window of Mrs Lewis's Leicester shop and set alight, destroying the entire stock of shoes.

The Japan-based Yokohama Rubber Company was forced to recall 300 tyres fitted on Mitsubishi jeeps in 1992 after protests from Muslims in Brunei and Saudi Arabia. They claimed the tyre tread pattern resembled the Arabic for 'Allah'. Company spokesman Akira Mikami said that the tyres were being replaced free of charge in Islamic countries and ran an apology in a magazine published by the Japanese Islamic association.

Yokohama blamed their computer for the costly coincidence. It had produced the tread design to maximise road safety. Later an unidentified gunman fired several shots at the entrance of a house owned by Hisaaki Suzuki, chairman of the company.

HAPPY BIRTHDAY . . . BIRTHDAY . . . BIRTHDAY . . .

ANGELA Johnson of Argyll has a strange pattern of births in her family. Since 1905 a female child has been born every thirty years on 20 May. Her grandmother, Mary Douglas, was born 20 May 1905, then her aunt Alfreda Douglas was born on 20 May 1935, followed by herself on 20 May 1965 and then her own daughter, Jemma Johnson, on 20 May 1995. Angela remarked: 'My daughter was actually due on 15 May, but I was in no doubt that she would not arrive until the twentieth!'

The three children born to Mr and Mrs E.H. Bisch of Santa Rosa, California, all have the same birthday. Peggy was born on 28 May 1954, Scott on 28 May 1958 and Kristine on 28 May 1959. Apparently the odds of three children in the same family being born on the same date are one in 28 million.

PIN PALS

TWO friends received the surprise of their lives when one of them went to the NatWest service till in Bedfont, Middlesex. As Jason Cook punched in his four figure PIN number, his friend Gary Burns stood beside him and recognised it as his own. The former soldiers had both been given the same number!

The bank said that the chances of two people being given the same number was 9,999–1. But for it to happen to friends with accounts at the same branch the odds were almost incalculable.

— ·4· —

REMARKABLE SURVIVORS

There are some amazing stories of people – and animals – who have cheated death, sometimes repeatedly, making a mockery of the laws of probability. Take the case of Joseph Figlock, for instance. Figlock was passing an apartment block in Detroit when he was knocked unconscious. A baby had fallen fourteen stories and landed on him. Both survived. One year later Figlock was passing the same apartment block – and once again he was hit by a falling child! He cheated death for the second time.

BROUGHT TO EARTH

LIGHTNING likes playing tricks with coincidence. On 4 July 1985 lightning struck the house of Scott Andres of Virgin Farm, Newfoundland, Canada. The following night his sister's house in North Bay, Ontario, was also struck. If that seems too much to believe, consider the following stories.

Harry Bowden from Durham survived two direct hits by

lightning. In 1968 a rake was torn from his hands, and a year later a bolt ripped his trousers, tore off his jacket, burned off the soles of his socks and split his shoes. Harry escaped with minor burns.

Retired forest ranger Roy Cleveland Sullivan of Waynesboro, Virginia, made it into the *Guinness Book of Records* because he survived being struck by lightning *seven* times. In 1942 he lost a big toenail when struck, in 1969 his eyebrows were blown off, his left shoulder was burned in 1970, and in 1972 his hair was set alight. After this incident he carried a gallon of water in his car. While out driving on 7 August 1973 a bolt came out of a small, low cloud and hit his head, making a hole in his hat and setting his hair on fire; it knocked him ten feet from his car and travelled down both legs, sending his left shoe flying. The other two instances were less memorable!

During thirty-six years as a ranger in the Shenandoah National Park Sullivan became quite a celebrity, although he never understood why lightning was attracted to him and, further, why it had not killed him. He once made the curious statement that he could see the lightning travelling towards him.

When he finally did die, it was by his own hand. On 28 September 1983, aged seventy-one, he shot himself and was finally earthed.

Aeschylus, the author of seventy ancient Greek tragedies, never ventured outside during storms because an oracle had warned him he would die by 'a blow from heaven'. He died in 456 BC whilst sitting outside on a sunny day in Gela, Sicily. An eagle, mistaking his bald head for a rock, dropped a huge tortoise on him to break its shell.

THE MOST REMARKABLE STORY
EVER TOLD?

IT is amazing how the results of one tragedy can be cured by another. Frederick Burdett, for instance, a seventy-one-year-old gold prospector dislocated his back after falling fifty feet in 1935. A few months later, on Christmas Eve, he was run over by a heavy oxcart. Not only did he survive the second accident, it cured his dislocation and he was able to walk free of pain once more.

This has got to be one of the most remarkable survival stories ever told – how an American woman with an incurable and degenerative condition made a miracle recovery.

In 1972 blonde, attractive, nineteen-year-old Mary Clamser had just started work as an air hostess when she became ill with severe abdominal pains and pins-and-needles in her legs. When the symptoms increased and she developed blurred vision and slurred speech, the doctors diagnosed multiple sclerosis. At that time she was newly engaged to be married and went from feeling on top of the world to the bottom. Within a short time she was confined to bed, and eventually Mary could only get around in a wheelchair.

The doctors said she would never walk again and that it was unlikely she would bear children – and, even if she did, Mary would be unable to care for them. MS attacks the nervous system, which then affects muscle operation. She decided to break off the engagement, but her fiancé Ron, was determined to make the best of it and they were duly married. With Ron's strength they took each day at a time and, indeed, brought up a family.

Over the years the disease was progressive, but intermittent. Mary had good times and bad, but as the years passed the good times became fewer and fewer. During 1992 she was almost permanently wheelchair bound. The disease not only had a severe impact on Mary but also on her family. Because of fatigue, she could not go out with them, missed school activities and found that her body was forcing her to become a different person. As time went by she became increasingly dependent on her family.

'Not only did I have to deal with the physical factor of losing more and more control over my body, there was also the emotional factor too of losing my active role in the family.'

As the disease progressed she could no longer operate the wheelchair any more and had to buy a motorised scooter. By 1992 it was obvious that the condition was in its final stages. She could not even get out of bed on her own, and mostly relied on her teenage sons to carry her to the bathroom. Mary found it a terrible existence.

'I was alive, but I was dead,' was how she put it.

The additional pressures took their toll on the family. Ron and Mary tried not to worry one another with their feelings, but the children were forever bickering.

'I saw my world come crashing down, but there wasn't anything I could do to stop it.'

Two years went by and the family adjusted as best they could. Then, on 17 August 1994, Oklahoma City was hit by a terrible electrical storm. The forecast was so bad that nineteen-year-old Ron junior stayed at home from college in case his mother was forced to evacuate the house. As the storm hit, it produced wind, rain, hail – and lightning.

Mary feared the electricity supply might be cut off because of the storm, leaving her in the dark, so she decided the best place for her to be was in the bathroom. While she was there, Mary used the toilet. Because of her disabilities, she hauled herself upright again on the metal shower door, then operated the flusher with her other hand. Just as she did this Mary saw a flash of lightning and thought 'there goes the satellite dish'. It lit up the whole bathroom, but she never heard the thunderclap.

Mary awoke in hospital. She had been struck by lightning. Now she was in excruciating pain as if someone was pouring fire down her back. She heard hospital staff discussing her condition and remarking that the paralysis in her legs was due to multiple sclerosis, not the lightning strike. But there was a change in Mary. For the first time in twenty-four years she could feel her legs . . .

'It was overwhelming. I was in shock and very agitated.'

Her doctor told her the apparent improvement would be transitory, and she would be back where she started in a month. It takes about thirty days, she was told, to recover from a lightning strike.

Once stabilised, Mary was allowed home, although she was still in excruciating pain. Then the burns started to come out. It felt as if her whole body were on fire. As the days passed the pain gradually subsided and Mary could still feel her legs. For a time she suffered short-term memory loss. On 12 September, three weeks after the lightning strike, Mary found herself in the kitchen and was frustrated because she could not remember why she had gone there. When her son walked in, he started laughing. Mary was standing up and using her hands!

Over the next few days she began to take a few steps. On the Friday of that week, when her husband came home from work, Mary walked down the path to meet him. She said to Ron 'I'm back,' and he almost had a heart attack.

Since then Mary's life has turned around. She can jog, run, drive a car again and even dance. As she puts it 'My family's enjoying a new mother and my husband has a new wife.'

What could have brought about this miraculous recovery? It

seems too complete for Mary to have gone into remission, which is highly unlikely anyway. Dr Bruce Hensel speculates that the lightning corrected whatever caused the multiple sclerosis. The disease affects the nervous system by stripping away the myelin sheath which carries the nerve impulses. Could the lightning have stimulated the cells responsible for making the myelin?

It is ironic that the lightning strike, which had the potential to kill Mary, became her saviour. Her physician, Dr Michael Moody, declared 'She's one of the luckiest people in the world.'

DEEP THROAT

CHRISTINE Barnett of Dyfed in Wales could not understand what was wrong with her twelve-month-old boxer dog Kizzy. She was losing weight and vomiting. The vet put the dog on a five-week course of tablets and took some blood samples, but the results were negative.

Unhappy with the animal's worsening condition, Christine took Kizzy to another vet for a second opinion. He felt a lump in her stomach and diagnosed cancer. Christine agreed that he should carry out an operation.

When the vet opened up Kizzy, he could scarcely believe his eyes. There, in her stomach, was a twelve-inch bread knife! Apparently the knife had disappeared at the same time Kizzy became ill, but no one had made the connection. It had slid down her throat, handle first, probably as she had licked a morsel of food from it. The handle and part of the blade ended up in Kizzy's stomach, and the rest of the blade lodged in her oesophagus. The dog made a full recovery!

LIFE'S RUFF FOR BULLIT

K IZZY did well escaping death once, but Bullit, the mongrel dog from America, has survived *six times*. It began when she was just six months old and Sharon DuVall's son, John, almost ran over her. Realising she was a stray, the family decided to keep her.

A year later the dog was accidentally shot by a hunter. Sharon cleaned out the wound and Bullit recovered. Next she was hit twice by cars. There were worries she might lose an eye, but Bullit pulled through. When she was X-rayed, the vet found more buckshot! She had been shot again and her owners had known nothing about it. Sharon was by now so worried Bullit might get fatally shot that she painted the dog's fur bright orange during the hunting season.

As if this was not enough, Bullit's next exploit led her to get hit by a train. She saw John on the other side of the tracks and ran over to him – right in the path of the engine. Her jaw was broken and she lost part of a paw, but made a good recovery. Again she was X-rayed, and once more buckshot was found. Sharon hoped that was the last of Bullit's death-defying stunts.

DOG GONE

T RIXIE, the Jack Russell terrier belonging to Mr and Mrs McManus, was not accustomed to the ground suddenly disappearing beneath her paws. The couple and their dog lived by the sea at Troon in Strathclyde, but in May 1996 went for a holiday on mainland Orkney. It was while they were walking on Whitaloo Point that the dog almost lost its life.

It was chasing rabbits, when, inexplicably, the dog discovered it had run out of land and plunged eighty feet over a cliff into the Atlantic. Trixie managed to swim to a rock and was later rescued by the Pentland coastguard, unharmed except for shock.

A BARK FOR HELP

EVERY so often a familiar tragic story makes its way into the newspapers. A toddler has been discovered drowned in an ornamental pond or the family's swimming pool. It only takes a minute while the mother has her back turned for the tragedy to occur. This would have been the fate of two-year-old Rhys Loram except he was destined to become 'one in a million'.

Rhys is the grandson of England speedway squad manager John Louis, and the son of speedway rider Mark Loram. In May 1986 it was bedtime for the toddler and he was changed into his favourite black and red Grand Prix pyjamas. He and Henka, the family's German shepherd, were inseparable friends, and Rhys wanted one last game with the dog before sleep. Joanne, his mother, relented, and the pair went out into the garden of their sixteenth-century farmhouse in Stowmarket, Suffolk.

Suddenly, from upstairs, Joanne heard Henka barking furiously and squealing in panic. Instinctively she thought the dog had hurt himself and rushed outside. What she saw was much worse. Rhys had fallen through a gap in the metal grid that covered the pond. He was upside down with his head and shoulders submerged, his legs sticking out into the air. Henka was going mad, clawing at the youngster, trying to dig him out.

Joanne hastily pulled the toddler out of the pond and he opened his eyes and coughed up some water. There was no doubt that, if it had not been for Henka, Rhys would have drowned. The dog was rewarded with an extra helping of his favourite – a packet of Opal Fruits.

BACK FROM THE DEAD

BY all the laws of nature Sean and Anne McNulty should be mourning the death of their baby son, Joshua. Instead they are celebrating his return to life after a serious accident in April 1996 that involved the whole family.

The McNultys were on holiday motoring near Great Yarmouth, Norfolk, when their Ford Escort collided with another car and rolled on its side into a water-filled dyke. With them were their other sons, Daniel, seven, and Andrew, six.

Mr McNulty escaped by kicking out the sun roof and then helped out other members of his family. It was then that he realised ten-month-old Joshua was not in the car. He had been sitting strapped into a child seat at the back, but now he was nowhere to be seen. At first Mr McNulty thought the child must be under the car, but he was not there. Then he waded around through the waist-deep water, but there was no sign of him.

Their luggage had spilled into the dyke and he kept picking up items of clothing, thinking they were Joshua. His wife was convinced the baby was dead. Then a woman on the bank shouted, 'He's behind you!' Joshua had been catapulted out of the car ten feet into the water. His father pulled him out by his cardigan on to the bank. The boy's face was pale and his lips were turning blue. There was no sign of life in him, he had stopped breathing. Mr McNulty said, 'I don't know what death looks like, but it looked as if he had already gone.' Little Joshua had drowned.

Alex Hardy, a passenger in the other vehicle, tried sticking his fingers down the child's throat to get the water out, but there was no response. While Mr McNulty started slapping Joshua on the back and carried out chest compressions, the other man did mouth-to-mouth resuscitation. Mr Hardy described what happened next.

'After I had breathed six or seven times into the baby's mouth, his eyes slowly opened and he coughed feebly, then more vigorously until he was crying.'

They still have no idea how he was thrown out of the car. Afterwards Mr McNulty, a trained first-aider, said, 'He has hardly got a mark on him, just a couple of grazes on his head. It is as if he has come back from the dead.'

Like Joshua McNulty, eighteen-month-old Jack Baker was strapped in a child seat when the car in which he was travelling hit another. It happened on the A69 at Warwick Bridge near Carlisle in June 1995. The seat was rear facing and situated in the back of the car. Somehow the head-on collision ripped the seat from its moorings and sent it hurtling through the windscreen – with the child still in it. The impact caused a third vehicle to be involved in the pile up.

When police and ambulance men arrived, they found Jack sitting in his chair, which now rested on the car bonnet. They were astonished to find him completely unharmed, even though several adults were taken to hospital with various injuries.

Toddlers seem to make a habit of surviving car accidents relatively unscathed. In July 1994 two-year-old Charlotte Donaldson from Nursling, Hampshire, was riding in the back of a friend's car with her mother, Dawn, when she decided to open the door. Somehow she had managed to unfasten the straps on her safety seat. Charlotte fell out and clung on to the sill as the car sped at forty miles per hour along a motorway. Then she disappeared beneath the back wheel of the car. A tanker travelling behind narrowly missed running over her.

Paula Searle, who was driving, said she felt a bump as her Austin Montego went over the little girl's leg. As the car stopped, Dawn Donaldson was convinced Charlotte was dead: 'I picked her up and you could see the tyre marks, but she only had cuts and bruises.' An X-ray examination showed she had a tiny crack in her ankle bone, but that was all.

SAVED BY 'COINCIDENCE'

PAULA Dixon was on a flight from Hong Kong to London in 1995 when she was struck down with something which should have killed her. She had a collapsed lung and a call was put out on the aircraft for any doctors. Not one, but two came forward – Professor Angus Wallace and Dr Tom Wong.

The presence of two doctors on a flight is not that surprising, but these were the ideal doctors for this particular emergency. Professor Wallace was not only an expert in accident surgery but he had also just finished a course which dealt with exactly this kind of crisis. Furthermore, Dr Wong just happened to have with him the textbook they needed to refer to in order to carry out the surgery which saved Paula's life – to worldwide acclaim.

BURIED ALIVE – AND LIVES

DOWN the years there have been many tragic stories of workmen buried alive while digging trenches. Almost invariably they die due to the crushing weight of soil and asphyxia. Who would have thought that someone buried under such horrendous conditions for more than an hour could survive?

In April 1995 Cunhai Gao, a Chinese-born geologist based at Cambridge University, was taking soil samples at a farm in Willingham. He was in a twenty-foot trench when it collapsed on top of him. Firemen were called to the scene. Using their hands and small trowels because they feared that a mechanical digger might seriously injure him, the firemen eventually uncovered Mr Gao. Since most of them fully expected to find a corpse they were amazed to discover that Mr Gao had not only survived his entombment but had suffered no serious injury other than a broken arm. Why wasn't he dead?

It transpired that, when the sides of the trench collapsed on top of him, Cunhai Gao was doubled up and his hard hat had slipped over his face, helping form an air pocket. How he survived an *hour* with so little air is still a mystery. All that concerns Cunhai Gao, however, is that he survived at all: 'When I saw the blue sky again, I thought my life was starting all over again. This is my second life now.'

THE EIGHT-MINUTE MIRACLE

MEDICAL science believes that if a human being stops breathing for more than three minutes irreversible brain damage occurs. What chance then would a small boy, starved of oxygen for *eight* minutes have of making any kind of recovery at all?

Nine-year-old Tony Wicks was playing on the canal side in Doncaster with his cousin, Joshua, in August 1995. When Tony fell in, Joshua ran to a nearby canal office and alerted Mr Bob Edwards. The alarm was logged at 4.48 pm.

Bob at once ran to the spot where the boy had disappeared, but there were no signs of him. He leapt into the cold water feet first and eventually found Tony on the bottom of the canal and hauled him to the bank. Bob, a qualified lifesaver, could feel no heartbeat and no pulse. To all intents and purposes the boy was drowned. But the fifty-seven-year-old was not one to give up and so he gave Tony the kiss of life. A minute later the lad coughed and opened his eyes. It was by this time 4.56 pm. The youngster went on to make a full recovery.

How was Tony able to survive? Doctors, dumfounded by the boy's return from death, speculated that the shock of the cold water slowed down his breathing and heartbeat so that hardly any of the oxygen already in his bloodstream was used. In effect, Tony was virtually in suspended animation.

THE OFF-SHORE REBEL

IT seemed a good idea at the time. Hospital porter Andrew Alsop offered to take his boss, Alan Davies, and Mr Davies's seven-year-old son, Aaron, out for a trip in his speedboat in May 1996. Soon after leaving the slipway at Sully, South Wales, the engine cut out and *Off-Shore Rebel* began to drift. When Mr Alsop tried using his mobile phone to call for help, he discovered the batteries were flat.

Darkness fell and a storm blew up. They knew there was even less chance of rescue now – at least until daylight. The little boy was becoming quite afraid, so Mr Alsop decided to take drastic action. Despite protestations from his boss, he jumped overboard and began swimming for the shore – a distance of about half a mile.

Fortunately he was a strong swimmer and, despite the storm, made it to the shore. There he contacted the coastguard, but Mr Alsop's ordeal was not yet over. The coastguard told him not to risk his life by going back, but he was still extremely concerned about his friend and the little boy. Andrew plunged back into the sea and, although extremely tired, made it back to the *Off-Shore Rebel* – half an hour ahead of the life boat!

MY LITTLE RUNAWAY

JERRY Simpson was a railway engineer working on a bridge in the Cascade Mountains, Washington, in 1886 when he faced – what seemed at the time – certain death. He looked up and saw a runaway North Pacific engine bearing down on him. Too near the centre of the bridge to run in either direction, he had only a few seconds to consider the alternatives: if he jumped over the parapet of the bridge, he might survive, but would almost certainly spend the rest of his life with crippling injuries, or he could lie down on the track and accept his fate. Choosing the latter course, he threw himself across the rails. The out-of-control engine left the track moments before crushing Simpson, cleared his body and then crashed into the gully below.

FREE FALL

STORIES of people falling thousands of feet from aircraft and surviving appear from time to time. By all accounts these free-fallers should die on impact, but in our unpredictable world, fortunately for them, this does not always happen. Like Russian fighter pilot Lieutenant I.M. Chisov, who fell 21,980 feet from his aircraft and lived.

Like many others, sales executive Alison Davis decided to parachute jump for charity. Encouraged by colleagues at work who agreed to sponsor her, Alison trained at the Skysports Paracentre in Bridlington, where she received tuition from qualified instructors. In September 1989 Alison flew to 3,500 feet and then jumped.

Almost as soon as she stepped out of the aircraft Alison knew she was in trouble. When she looked up, the parachute lines were twisted so the canopy was hardly open. As she plunged towards the ground the twenty-four-year-old realised she was too low to use her emergency chute and panicked. This probably saved her life, because she fainted and was unconscious when she hit the ground.

Alison survived the fall with a broken pelvis and shoulder, two broken bones in her neck and a fractured jaw. Experts said that, if she had not fainted, her body would have been rigid on impact and she would have died. In an unconscious state her body was relaxed and better able to absorb the shock.

In June 1994 another parachutist was saved from certain death – by a tree. John Goodyear from Liverpool was performing with other members of the Black Knights freefall team at a school fête in June when the accident happened. Crowds watched in horror as John spun out of control when a daredevil stunt went wrong. He plunged towards the ground and at the last second his fall was broken by a beech tree. He escaped with a broken leg.

Here is a story of a parachutist who 'fell' *up* 6,000 feet. Rick Collins was practising for the 1982 Commonwealth Games opening ceremony in Brisbane at the time. He jumped through a thundercloud and, just after his main parachute opened, turbulence sucked him up 6,000 feet. Lightning zipped around him and he was bombarded by hailstones. Afterwards he told reporters: 'I knew these cloud formations could extend up to 25,000 feet, and at that height I would pass out through lack of oxygen. There was also the danger that I would suffer serious injuries from the hailstones that were smashing into me.'

Rick decided to release his parachute at 12,000 feet and free fall to a safer altitude. He wrapped his arm around his face to protect himself from the hail which was coming up at him. He kept an eye on his altimeter. When he was down to 1,500 feet, he pulled the ripchord on his emergency parachute and landed safely in a field five miles from the stadium target.

What happened to Steve Trebble when he took part in a charity parachute jump gave a whole new meaning to the term 'free fall'. Steve and two other members of the Life Guards Regiment Parachute Display Team had arranged to do a sponsored parachute jump in April 1984 for a charity seeking to preserve mountain gorillas.

The team decided to dress up in gorilla suits for the event and were planning to perform a mid-air manoeuvre known as canopy stacking. In this manoeuvre the three parachutists join up together. Steve and his colleagues were in confident mood that day. The weather conditions were good and they had a great time larking around in their gorilla suits. They made all their checks and were ready to go. It was almost routine.

The aircraft took off and flew to 3,500 feet. On the ground

were reporters and a camera crew to record the unusual event. Steve Trebble and Dave Speed jumped first, and their parachutes opened without problem. As planned, the two men docked and waited for the third man, Barry Henderson, to complete the manoeuvre. Barry jumped and came up behind the other two, but then something went wrong. Maybe the angle was not right, but Barry hit their canopies and the impact knocked out the air, causing them to collapse.

The formation was thrown into disarray. Barry recovered his stability, while 'Speedy' released himself from his main canopy and successfully activated his reserve. Meantime Steve Trebble attempted to do the same, but his reserve wrapped itself around his leg, sending him into free fall, dropping like a stone towards the ground. As he began spinning, Steve managed to release his leg, but the lines were caught in his backpack, preventing it from opening.

'I remember two things vividly. One was a flash, which was my life rushing by. It took only milliseconds, but I knew exactly what it was. Then, as I span towards the ground, I saw an image of my wife following me whichever direction I faced. I screamed out her name.'

Steve was still struggling, trying to free his reserve parachute. The last thing he remembered was Dave Spencer, one of the ground crew, shouting 'put your head up'. Then there was green grass and nothing for a while.

'The next thing I remember is people screaming and somebody saying, "Don't move." Joyce, who's a nurse, was not allowed to touch me. I was in absolute agony around my chest, head and shoulders. So I wriggled my feet and they moved. At least I wasn't paralysed – but until then most people thought I was dead!'

An ambulance arrived and, followed by a film crew, Steve

was taken to hospital. There he was given twelve X-rays. Remarkably, every bone in his body was intact. Despite falling several thousand feet on to hard ground, apart from bruising and a lot of soreness, Steve Trebble was in good condition.

'Everybody's jaw dropped. No one could believe it. I asked the doctor if they were going to keep me in. He said no, I would be all right. The media finished interviewing me and then I just walked out.'

Steve was driven back to the airfield. When he walked into the canteen, there was a deathly hush. As he passed Joyce, she said, 'I've seen a miracle today.' There were no cheers or frivolity, everyone was too stunned. Most people thought he must have broken his back at least. Later that night he went to a local pub; by now the shock had worn off and the celebrations began.

Within two weeks Steve was up in the air doing another jump, and a month later he was taking part in the World Parachute Display Championships.

— · 5 · —

DEADLY COINCIDENCES

One-in-a-million events intrude upon all aspects of our lives. They can bring about happiness, humour, farce, pathos and even death. Here are some from the darker side. . .

KEEP DEATH OFF THE ROAD

IN 1975 the strange death of two brothers was reported in Bermuda. Erskine Lawrence Ebbin was knocked off his moped and killed by a taxi in Hamilton in July. It was the same taxi with the same driver, carrying the same passenger, that had killed his brother Neville on the same moped – precisely a year earlier. The brothers were both seventeen when they died and met their deaths on the same street.

Mopeds may be a fairly common form of transport, but a snowmobile featured in the separate deaths of a man and his wife in Lewis, near Syracuse, in the state of New York. Michael Staring died on 18 February 1996 when he misjudged the distance between a fence and an open gate. The glare of the sun caused him to drive his snowmobile into barbed wire and he received fatal injuries. Two years previously, in January 1994, his wife had met her death when a car collided with the snowmobile she was driving.

On the morning of 19 January 1991 nineteen-year-old Cristina Veroni was killed when her car was struck by a train on the Via Cartoccio level crossing in Reggio Emilia, in northern Italy. Local railway crossings in Italy are unmanned and have no protective barrier. This particular crossing was near a bend set in a flat landscape, where the sun can be blinding.

Almost five years later, on the morning of Wednesday 8 November 1995, Cristina's father, Vittorio Veroni, was killed at the same crossing. His Renault 21 was hit by a train and dragged along the track on a similar bright, sunny morning.

Suggestions that he had taken his own life at the place where his daughter had died were refuted by his family and the train driver, Domenica Serafino. It was believed that, like his daughter, he had been blinded by the sun, and his actions were hindered by a plaster cast he wore around his chest following a workplace accident.

When Kim Pilling, a reporter for the *Burnley Express*, was sent to cover a tragic accident in July 1995, he did not learn until some time later that two of the victims were his parents.

The accident occurred when a van driver had a heart attack and mounted a pavement, ploughing into Rodney and Marie Pilling, killing them. At the scene of the accident the police would not give Kim the names of the victims until relatives had been notified. The reporter did, however, speak to the relatives of a third victim, Mrs Ivy Waddington, but he was still none the wiser as to the identity of the middle-aged couple.

Later he tried to telephone his parents, who lived near by, to see if they knew who was involved, but he assumed they were out when no one answered. It was while he was watching a brief report on television that he began to grow suspicious. Then the news was broken to him, he commented, 'When I was out there, I just never knew.'

DON'T LOOK NOW!

THE film that Julie Christie starred in was to have real life echoes six years later. *Don't Look Now*, released in 1973, was based on a Daphne du Maurier story. The film is atmospheric and filled with tension, revolving around the parents of a young child played by Donald Sutherland and Julie Christie. The family live in a country house with a shallow pond in its grounds. In the opening scenes we see the child drown in a few inches of water. Christie stands on the bank watching, as her co-star wades into the water to retrieve the body. The film explores the idea that the child comes back to haunt them.

In March 1979 Julie Christie drove out to her farmhouse in Wales, which had a duck pond. The house was occupied at the time by a young couple and their son. A macabre replay of the drowning scene in the film was about to be re-enacted, but this time for real. The two-year-old was discovered in the pond and Julie Christie found herself standing on the bank while the mother waded into the water and carried the dead child out.

As an added twist, Constable Frank Podmore gave evidence at the inquest. He bore the same name as one of the pioneers of the Society for Psychical Research – who was also found drowned in a pond.

DESTINED FOR DEATH

WHAT are we to make of the strange series of events which dogged two American presidents who were elected 100 years apart? Abraham Lincoln was elected the country's sixteenth president in 1860. He was a popular leader who championed the rights of the underprivileged, and took a leading role in the abolition of slavery. History books depict him as one of the greatest presidents. He had just begun his second term when, on 14 April 1865, he was shot dead by actor John Wilkes Booth as he sat in a theatre.

Nineteen presidents later John F. Kennedy was elected in 1960. He too was a great defender of civil rights and was well loved by ordinary people in many countries as well as respected by politicians across the political divide. The similarities do not end there.

Both men were elected to Congress in '47 and competed for vice-presidential nominations in '56. Kennedy and Lincoln were in their thirties when they married pretty, twenty-four-year-old brunettes who lost children while in the White House and who spoke fluent French. Both men were assassinated on a Friday. Kennedy *and* Lincoln were shot dead while sitting next to their wives. Lincoln had a secretary named Kennedy, and Kennedy had one called Lincoln. Kennedy advised Lincoln not to go to the theatre, and Lincoln advised Kennedy not to go to Dallas.

President Kennedy was killed whilst riding in a Ford Lincoln car. Booth shot Lincoln in a theatre and fled into a warehouse; Oswald shot Kennedy from a warehouse and fled into a theatre. Lee Harvey Oswald, like Booth, had a three-part name and both were killed before they could be brought to trial. Booth was born in 1839 and Oswald in 1939. Finally, Lincoln and Kennedy were succeeded by presidents born 100 years apart (1808 and 1908), both southerners and both named Johnson.

Abraham Lincoln was the second member of his family to die by an assassin's bullet: the other was his grandfather – also named Abraham, both had a wife named Mary and both had a son named Thomas. Several years after John Kennedy's murder, his brother Bobby was also shot dead.

A TALE OF TWO MURDERS

CAN there be a causal link between two murders 157 years apart or is it 'mere' coincidence?

On 27 May 1817 twenty-year-old Mary Ashford was found murdered in the village of Erdington, five miles outside Birmingham. On 27 May 1974 Barbara Forest, also aged twenty, was strangled and left in a ditch not far from the children's home in Erdington where she worked. Both girls were raped and both were nurses. There were a number of other similarities too.

In 1817 and 1974 Whit Monday fell on 26 May. Both girls had visited a friend that evening to change into a dress to go to a dance. After each murder a man was arrested, and in each instance his name was Thornton – Abraham Thornton and Michael Thornton respectively. At both murder trials the accused was acquitted owing to lack of evidence.

HIGHLAND HOSPITALITY

ON 26 May 1994 *The Scotsman* published a letter from an Australian tourist expressing his appreciation of a small Highland guesthouse:

> Just to prove that Scotland is a home away from home for the weary traveller, we found a bed and breakfast near Kyle of Lochalsh run by a Mr and Mrs Macmillan at Grianan House. We didn't want to leave. This is what we came all the way from Australia to find. We will be back next year. Thank you Donald and Zena, also young Donald, for restoring our faith in Scotland and the Scots.

That *same day* the following news story appeared in the *West Highland Free Press*: 'An Inverinate man appeared in private at Dingwall Sheriff's Court on Monday, charged with the murder of hillwalker Helen Torbet, who disappeared last summer. He is Donald MacMillan, 32, son of the owners of Grianan House, Inverinate – the guesthouse where Mrs Torbet had been staying while on holiday.'

FATAL ATTRACTION

PRISCILLA Brayboy of Houston, Texas, suspected her husband of having a lover and decided to surprise him. She waited until he left home in his grey Volvo and then went looking for him with a friend.

On spotting what she thought was her husband's car parked in a driveway, she knocked on the door of the house and tried to barge her way in. One of the occupants, alarmed at what was

happening, fired off a shotgun and killed her. The friend ran
down the street screaming and then noticed Mr Brayboy's grey
Volvo parked in another drive.

JUST DESERTS

IN 1893 Henry Ziegland of Honey Grove, Texas started a chain
of events which was to culminate in his death twenty years
later. After being jilted, his girlfriend went and killed herself.
Her brother blamed Ziegland and decided to avenge his sister
by shooting him. But the bullet only grazed his head and buried
itself in a tree. Thinking he had killed him, the brother went off
and committed suicide.

In 1913 Ziegland decided to cut down the tree which had the
bullet in it. The job proved tougher than he thought, so he
decided to use dynamite instead. The explosion sent the old bullet into Ziegland's head, killing him.

Francis Wearne, a retired seventy-three-year-old businessman, went pheasant shooting on Dartmoor in 1973 with an older
friend. A bird appeared and, as it flew overhead, Mr Wearne
fired off his gun. Somehow the shot was deflected by the bird
and hit the hunter in the face. Shortly afterward Mr Wearne's
eye became bruised and swollen. He was admitted to Torbay
Hospital for observation, but died during the night. Apparently
a pellet had entered the eyelid, causing a blood clot in the brain.
His widow commented, 'It was a chance in a million.'

A GRAVE COINCIDENCE

THE poet and novelist Robert Graves was connected with three coincidences that revolved around his book *The White Goddess*, published in 1946. Graves was overwhelmed with a desire to start the work while completing *The Golden Fleece*. He was prompted by a number of references to 'Ngame', an African moon goddess, which kept coming his way in a variety of guises. Indeed, the book revolved around the premise of an ancient global religion rooted in the worship of a pagan goddess.

The first publisher to reject the manuscript died from a heart attack. A second not only rejected it but also made rude comments. That publisher hanged himself from a tree in his garden wearing ladies lingerie. Graves sent it to a third publisher, the poet T.S. Eliot. Fortunately for Graves – and Eliot – he accepted it. That same year the publisher was awarded the Order of Merit.

Robert Graves saw all of this as having some deep underlying meaning. Was it the goddess at work or Graves's own unconscious influencing the external world? He wrote: 'Chains of more than coincidence happen so often in my life that I am forbidden to call them supernatural. I must call them a habit.'

Of the *White Goddess* affair he said somewhat flippantly: 'Very well, put it down to coincidence.'

— ·6· —
STRANGE SYNDROMES
AND
MEDICAL CONDITIONS

Despite extensive study and mapping of the human body over many centuries, it still manages to perplex and amaze science with one-in-a-million syndromes and extreme medical conditions.

JOANNA'S SYNDROME

LITTLE Joanna Harris from Guildford in Surrey really is one in a million. She has a medical condition which is unique, which includes aspects of Lupus, Cryoglobulinaemia and Bechet's Syndrome. Doctors have labelled it 'Joanna's Syndrome'. Five-year-old Joanna simply calls it 'Jack Frost'. Her parents noticed there was something wrong shortly after Joanna was born, as Susan, her mother, explained.

'She became ill within twenty-four hours of leaving hospital. Her temperature raged, she came out in a rash and had many of the symptoms of pneumonia and meningitis. We didn't know what was wrong so she went back into hospital.'

There medical staff stabilised her temperature and she returned to normal. It was some time before anyone realised that it was the cold which set off her condition. Doctors eventually discovered exactly what happens to Joanna when the temperature drops.

If it is too cold for Joanna, the blood cools, her proteins react and silt up her system. This causes a reaction that results in fever, blisters and frostbite. At its worst her extremities ulcerate, putting her life in danger.

Joanna's condition is controlled by a cocktail of immune suppressant drugs. Ideally the family would like to move to a warmer climate, where Joanna would have a better quality of life. Here she goes to a local school when the weather is warm. At the moment there is no cure for her condition.

STONES THROW AWAY

THE McNabs were a family of losers. Their huge sizes attracted stares and cruel taunts from children in the street. For Robert McNab breakfast consisted of five fried eggs, bacon, five slices of buttered toast, three doughnuts and coffee with cream. It was no wonder he weighed 28st 8lb, and kids pointed to his huge stomach and jeered, 'He's pregnant!'

The rest of the family possessed equal appetites. They would spend all day eating vast quantities of cakes, burgers, chips, fried chicken and ice-cream. In fact most of their money was spent on food. Weightwise they also followed in Dad's footsteps. Mrs Jennifer McNab weighed 17st 4lb, elder son Robert junior 20st, Leonard 17st 12lb and daughter Heather 16st 6lb.

Mr and Mrs McNab finally decided something had to give, and their grown-up children agreed. The family, who run a nursing home in New Hampshire, USA, followed a strict eating regime drawn up by their doctor and, coupled with daily exercises, lost an amazing forty-three stone between them!

After seventeen months, in May 1996, the new sleek McNabs weighed in at the following: Dad 12st 8lb, Mum 9st 11lb, Robert 11st 11lb, Leonard 14st 4lb and Heather 9st 4lb. Mr McNab now weighs less than he did when he was eleven years old.

ONE IN THE EYE

THIS curious story was written up in the September 1979 issue of the medical journal *Archives of Opthalmology*. It concerns a seven-year-old South African boy named Julian Fabricus. He fell down in a field while chasing butterflies, and afterwards his eye was inflamed and smarting.

His mother took him to see a doctor in Worcester, who could not find the source of the discomfort and prescribed some ointment. Several days later the smarting went and all was forgotten. A year went by, then Julian complained that his left eye itched and his vision was blurred. His father inspected the eye and noticed a white object lodged in the cornea, near the pupil.

Julian was taken to see oculist Dr Cornelius Kooy, who was amazed at what he found: 'I saw what looked like a grass seed which had sprouted and grown two little leaves.' The seedling was about an eighth of an inch long and pure white. The case was referred to Dr Solomon Abel, a top eye specialist in Cape Town. He removed the seed in a thirty-minute operation. A botanist indentified the invader as one of the family of *compositae*, which includes chrysanthemums, thistles and daisies.

In his report, Dr Abel concluded that the boy's cornea had been punctured when he fell in the field and the seed had found its way through the wound and into the iris. There it remained dormant for a year and then started growing. Julian made a full recovery.

UNWELL AT HOLLINWELL

WHAT happened at the Hollinwell Show held on Sunday 13 July 1980 that caused hundreds to collapse on the ground? The event was held on fields near Kirkby in Ashfield, Nottinghamshire. It was to feature a competition between junior brass and marching bands, many of whom had travelled there in coaches to arrive for the 9.30 am start. The children gathered on the fields for an inspection parade to begin at 11 am. Shortly before mid-day disaster struck. Over 200 children and several adults collapsed like ninepins.

Terry Bingham, one of the show's organisers, described what happened. 'We were ready for the display when one or two children collapsed. Then a few more went, and a few more. We called off the event, but others fell as they came out of the arena. Then spectators started dropping.'

Another witness said: 'Some kids were catching their friends as they fell, and then they were falling themselves. No one could understand what was happening – it was like a battlefield with bodies everywhere.'

Altogether 259 people were ferried by dozens of ambulances to four area hospitals and examined. Nine children, including two babies, were detained overnight. The victims variously complained of fainting, dizziness, vomiting, trembling, weakness, numbness and a metallic taste in the mouth.

One of the initial explanations was food poisoning. But tests on fast food, ice-cream and drinks available at the show proved negative. Then someone suggested that a cloud of poisonous insecticide was responsible, but investigation ruled that out too. Then someone hit on the idea of 'mass hysteria'.

It was suggested that hysteria had overtaken everyone after seeing a few genuinely exhausted children collapse. Fourteen-year-old Petula Merriman said: 'We were on the field in full uniform for an inspection. I've never had to stand to attention that long before. As we marched off I grabbed for my drum, but just fell to the floor. My friends were collapsing all around me.' A ten-year-old by the name of Kerry Elliot said she suddenly went weak with stomach pains and then fainted.

But those who were there did not accept the psychological explanation. Certainly it could not account for the two babies since they were too young to be aware of what was going on. Some of the adults were affected while accompanying their children to hospital. The organisers said that the conditions for such a phenomenon did not exist that day. There was little tension – most people were relaxed – and it was far from hot, as a number of people wore coats. Terry Bingham said there was a cover-up by the authorities: 'I had chest pains. It was like nerve gas poisoning.'

No one was able to come up with the definitive answer as to why 259 apparently healthy people should suddenly collapse.

MAGNETIC PERSONALITIES

THERE are some people who apparently have magnetic properties that allow metallic objects to stick to their skin. Frank McKinstry of Joplin, Missouri, is one of the earliest 'magnetic' people on record. His powers were particularly strong in the mornings, and he spent most of that time frantically shuffling around lest he became fixed to the ground. This was not always possible to avoid and sometimes Frank had to ask for assistance to yank his legs free.

One of the most impressive cases is that of the Russian militia patrolman Nikolai Suvorov. He has demonstrated his powers many times before sceptics and television cameras, and is quite remarkable. He can apparently generate powers that can cause even heavy articles like frying pans and electric irons to stick to his body.

Magnetic people might be one in a million but, relatively speaking, they are not rare. In 1991 Bulgaria's Sofia Press Agency reported that over 300 people had shown up to take part in a contest to see who could keep the most and the heaviest objects fixed to their bodies the longest.

Erika zu Stirnberg from Bochum, Germany, was impressed by a television programme about a magnetic Russian woman and, as a joke, decided to put a spoon against her chest. It stayed there. Unbelieving, she emptied the contents of her cutlery drawer and one by one placed forks, knives and spoons on her body – where they remained. Do you have a hidden magnetic personality?

JONATHAN'S CAR REMAINS STATIC

JONATHAN Rainey stores up so much static electricity that he causes problems wherever he goes. The young man from County Antrim, Northern Ireland, first noticed the phenomenon at school when all the digits on his calculator went crazy. As he left school and started a job the effects became more dramatic.

'One of my worst moments came when my mobile phone blew up and then the car stopped all within fifteen seconds, leaving me totally stranded. I could never guarantee that I would be able to turn up anywhere on time and eventually lost my job.'

Jonathan's new Rover 100 Kensington repeatedly broke down. In three months the car spent more time in the garage than on the road. Mechanics thought the trouble lay in a faulty immobiliser and gave him a replacement vehicle. But the new car broke down twenty-two times in under four months.

Apparently the fault was due to the immobiliser: Jonathan's static electricity was confusing the signal from the remote hand set to the car. The problem was solved when he began driving a Renault Clio – which does not have an immobiliser.

Although relatively rare, there are a number of cases of people who affect electrical equipment in this way. Mrs R. Heath of Balham, London, wrote to the *Daily Mirror* in October 1973 describing her problem:

> I seem to have the knack of switching off electrical gadgets without even touching them! During my holidays, for example, I tried to dry my hands in the hot air machine in a ladies loo – only to find that it turned itself off, although it worked for everyone else. I even took my rings and shoes off, but it made no difference. It's the same story with automatic ticket machines on the Underground. They always reject my ticket. I also have a funny effect on transistor radios, which go static when I walk past.

These effects occur so often that Mrs Heath's friends have nicknamed her 'Spooky'.

WIDE AWAKE FOR THIRTY YEARS

SEÑORA Ines Fernandez was reported in 1973 as not having slept a wink for thirty years. On 8 July 1943 she was standing at the door of her cottage in Sierra de Fuentes in south-west Spain, watching a religious procession. She yawned and felt a searing pain in her head, since when she has never slept, despite taking thousands of pills and medicines, and consulting numerous doctors.

The old lady described agonising nights, sitting in an arm-chair next to her sleeping husband, praying for the morning to come. During this time she was treated by Dr Pablos Abril, a neurosurgeon. He commented that he had never seen a case like it before. The doctor described her condition as chronic colesistites and total insomnia. That area of the brain respon-sible for sleep appeared to be permanently damaged.

A London neurologist said that cases of this kind were extremely rare, but thought the origin might be more psycho-logical than physiological. Whatever the cause for Señora Fernandez's permanent insomnia, it raises the question – do we really need sleep at all?

SLEEPWALKER

WHEN schoolboy Mark Henderson went to bed on 16 September 1973 he expected to wake up in his bedroom. Instead the fourteen-year-old found himself forty feet up, perched on the roof of his house in Burnley, Lancashire. Dressed in his pyjamas and fast asleep, he had apparently climbed out of his attic bedroom through a tiny window and then walked ten feet down wet, slippery slates to the edge of the roof which overlooked the back yard. Neighbours saw him and alerted the emergency services. Mark was rescued by firemen and returned to bed none the worse for wear.

AMPHIBIAN BOY

HERE is a curious account which came out of the Basti district of Uttar Pradesh, India in February 1973. One afternoon a priest out walking on the banks of the River Kuano came across a strange sight. He saw a naked boy who apparently could walk on the surface of the water. At one point the boy dived in, brought out a large fish and then lay on his back, eating it, as he drifted down stream.

The priest returned to the village and told the story. When he described the boy, a woman called Somni said she thought it might be her son, Ramchandra, who was carried away by the river when he was only one. Another villager saw him a few days later and, although there was considerable local interest, sightings of the wonder boy dried up for several years.

Then, in May 1979, Somni spotted him lying in a field. As she crept nearer she recognised a birthmark on his back, but he then awoke and fled. After that the villagers took turns watching for him, and eventually captured the boy. He was virtually hairless and his black skin had a greenish tinge. After escaping back to the river, he became less reserved and accepted bowls of spinach soaked in water from the villagers. His favourite food was raw meat, fish, frogs, leafy vegetables, gourds and red chillies.

Word spread and people arrived from across the region to see the 'amphibian boy' in action. Hundreds, including police officials and journalists, watched him walk, run and recline on the surface of the river, and stay submerged for much longer than is normal. One of the main puzzles is how he was not attacked by the many crocodiles that live in the Kuano.

— · 7 · —

IN COLD PRINT

There is a saying that you should never commit anything to writing you might later regret. In the cases cited here, if the writers had not published their words, we would not have known of such wonderful coincidences!

SPELLBOUND

FORMER opera singer Jackie Nally lived and worked in Sydney, Australia in the 1960s. It was there that she met her future husband, who was British. Things did not go as they planned, so the couple decided to move back to England. Their British friends in Sydney subscribed to the *Observer* and they brought round a pile of old newspapers to help Jackie with the packing.

Back in England, they stayed at the Tooting home of the friends who had given them the papers. They liked the area so much that they registered with a local lettings agency. While walking in the area, they spotted a house that was up for rent which immediately appealed to them. In due course the couple secured a lease on the house and moved in.

Whilst unpacking her crockery, Jackie noticed an article on one of the sheets of newspaper. It was about a white witch named Mrs Bone, who lived at 120 Trinity Road, Tooting. Jackie gasped and called out to her husband. They had just moved into 120 Trinity Road – the same house formerly occupied by Mrs Bone!

TWO WEDDINGS AND A NEWSPAPER

HERE are two almost identical stories from opposite ends of the country, both set during World War II.

George Rolls met his future wife, Jean, at work in 1939. She left school at seventeen and joined the Electricity Board as his assistant. Love blossomed. As the war developed, Jean volunteered to join the Wrens, and George later joined the Intelligence Corps. In the summer of 1944 they became engaged. At that time she was stationed at Besty Park near Woburn Abbey and he was training in Yorkshire.

Finally he was given his orders. They were sending him to Indo-China. He travelled down to Besty Park to talk to Jean. She agreed they should be married as soon as possible. They had the conversation on the Wednesday, and by Saturday they were getting married at a church in Brentwood, Essex. The couple spent five 'blissful' days in Cornwall on honeymoon before George was sent out to Indo-China on 16 February.

It was during his stay in the holding camp in India that he obtained a day pass to go into Bombay. Tropical fruits were a rarity in Britain, so George was thrilled to buy a pineapple and some bananas from a local market. The bananas were wrapped in newspaper.

When he returned to camp and unwrapped his treasures, he was surprised to see that the paper was a copy of the Brentwood local. How on earth had it got to India? He was the only chap from Brentwood aboard the ship which had transported his regiment there. George was even more astounded when he saw it was the edition which contained the announcement of his wedding!

Lawrence Hewitt also met his bride to be when she was seventeen. They met in Wakefield Park in Yorkshire. They got engaged in 1940 and were married on 13 June 1941. The wedding had been brought forward before Lawrence was sent to the Middle East. He was at sea for seven weeks, travelling down to Cape Town and up the Red Sea to Egypt as part of the allied military build up for the North African campaign.

During his time in the desert many of the troops suffered from dysentry. It was in early October that Lawrence saw a prize bit of newspaper blowing past. Such paper was precious, so he grabbed it and found it was his local newspaper the *Wakefield Express*! But it wasn't any edition. On the page was a picture of his wedding . . .

THE MAN WHO FOUND HIMSELF

BUILDER David Randall was carrying out some work on a kitchen extension in Newham when he came face to face – with David Randall. He lifted up some lino and saw a picture of himself on the front page of the *Sunday Express* dated 16 July 1950. It showed a four-year-old boy with tousled hair and scruffy clothes holding hands with a little girl.

It described how the boy had saved the life of his friend Norma McAdam when she was drowning in a pond. Their mothers were pea-picking on a farm near Canterbury and the children were playing when it happened. Now, by 'coincidence', thirty-four years later, he was dramatically reminded of the incident.

BACK TO FRONT

WHEN ten-year-old Vicky Wilmore from Gorton, Manchester complained of a headache on 12 October 1994, it had consequences no one could have imagined. She began writing upside down and back to front. Although she could read her own work without hesitation, no one else could. This caused her a deep sense of frustration at school, and none of the experts who examined Vicky could provide a diagnosis. As the disorder became more severe her writing degenerated into unintelligible squiggles.

One of the ways in which Vicky sought to escape her problems was by following the exploits of her favourite football team, Manchester United. On 27 September 1995 they played Rotor Volgograd in the IEFA Cup. At one point during the match on television she became so excited that she jumped out of her seat and fell backwards, hitting her head on a coffee table.

The following day Vicky could read and write properly again. Dr Isabella Tweedle, senior clinical medical officer for child health with the Mancunian Community Health Trust, was astounded. She said: 'I have never come across anything like it before and neither has anyone that I know of.'

ON THE GULAG

WHILE in the Dmitrovak Prison, the Russian writer Alexander Solzhenitsyn recorded a strange incident for his future novel *The Gulag Archipelago*.

A fellow prisoner, the astronomer Kozayev, attempted to keep himself sane by spending his time working out a new physics formula. At a certain stage technical information was required to which he did not have access. The prison library only contained Communist propaganda. A book – any book – was issued to each prisoner every ten days and then exchanged.

Kozayev, extremely frustrated and depressed, prayed fervently for the information. Half an hour later the guards came to change the books. The book he was given was *The Theory of Astrophysics*, the very volume he needed. Somehow he knew he would not have the usual ten days to absorb its contents and spent the next forty-eight hours gleaning all the relevant material. At the end of that time an inspector called and, upon seeing the volume, had it immediately confiscated.

— ·8· —

SEEING DOUBLES

Coincidence can bring together lost twins and siblings and inflict on similar individuals parallel lives – and deaths. One can appreciate that some similarities of behaviour in identical twins are due to innate conditioning, but that does not explain how they can have accidents on the same day, or marry and divorce partners with the same names. Equally intriguing are the doubles created by Fate and coincidence.

THE KING AND I

In July 1900 King Umberto I of Italy was dining one night in a restaurant when he found his attention drawn towards the owner. The man bore a striking resemblance to himself, and they even shared the same name. More was to follow when the two men fell into conversation. Apparently they had been born on the same day and had married women with the same name.

The two men instantly developed a mutual admiration for one

another. It was as if they were brothers. King Umberto invited his new friend to attend an atheletics event with him, but he failed to arrive. While the games were in progress, the disappointed King sent one of his attendants to find out where he was. The servant returned to report that the restaurant owner had been killed that morning in a shooting accident. Shortly after receiving this devastating news, an assassin in the crowd pointed a gun at the King and shot him dead. The men's lives had run parallel right to the end.

JUST A NUMBER

A computer mix-up which gave two American women the same social security number was responsible for highlighting a further series of incredible coincidences. Patricia Kern of Colorado and Patricia di Biasi of Oregon were brought together by the blunder. The women discovered they had both been born Patricia Ann Campbell with fathers called Robert. They were born on the same date too: 13 March 1941. Both Patricias married military men in 1959 within eleven days of one another, and had children aged nineteen and twenty-one. They also shared an interest in painting with oils, had studied cosmetics and worked as book-keepers.

SIDE BY SIDE

TWO postal workers, Yvette Richardson and James Austin, worked side by side with one another in Philadelphia for two years before learning that they were sister and brother. The woman who put two and two together in June 1995 was shop steward Barrie Bowens.

Austin had told her that his father had died young. He had never known his mother because his parents had split up a few months after his birth. Bowens asked for the name of his mother, and he told her it was 'Veronica Potter'. Lights started flashing in the shop steward's head because she knew that was also the name of Richardson's mother. She told Richardson, who then noticed the physical similarities between her co-worker and an old picture of her father.

It was thirty-three years earlier that the children had been separated. Austin had been brought up by his paternal grand-parents in North Philadelphia, while Richardson lived with her mother in South Philadelphia. They had gone to school within blocks of one another and, despite the total lack of contact, both had studied accounting and both had ended up on the 4 pm shift at the post office, despite there being 4,100 employees.

MARRIED ON THE REBOUND

Is it possible to marry the same woman twice although on each occasion the bride is a different person? That is apparently what happened when Kim Carpenter married Krickitt for the second time in May 1996 – and they were not even divorced.

Krickitt Papas and Kim Carpenter 'met' over the telephone in September 1992. She was a representative for a Californian sportswear company, and he was the baseball coach for the New Mexico Highlands University. By January they were talking on the phone five hours a week. Eventually, after exchanging photographs, Kim invited Krickitt to Las Vegas to see his team play. They were married on 18 September 1993.

After honeymooning on Maui, they settled in New Mexico, where Krickitt found work as an exercise technician in a hospital. On 24 November 1993 – the day before Thanksgiving – their idyll came to a violent end. A pickup truck smashed into Krickitt's new Ford Escort on Interstate 40. Kim suffered broken ribs, a punctured lung, concussion, bruising to his heart muscle, and his nose and an ear were almost torn off. As if this was not bad enough, Krickitt received a massive head injury.

The doctors at Gallup, New Mexico hospital were convinced she would die. She was airlifted 130 miles to the University of New Mexico Hospital in Albuquerque, where her condition stabilised, although Krickitt was expected to remain in a vegetative state.

She emerged from coma around Christmastime and was as helpless as a newborn babe. Slowly her brain recovered and she learned how to walk again, but parts of her memory had been lost completely. She thought Richard Nixon was still president and all memory of the last few months had gone. When a nurse asked her, 'Who's your husband?', she replied, 'I'm not married.'

Kim pushed her to regain her fitness, but she rejected him, a stranger, and told him to go away. But patiently he persevered as she struggled to make sense of the wedding ring on her finger. When Krickitt returned home, she hoped the familiar surroundings would jog her memory, but the apartment, like the wedding photos, seemed to belong to another person. When she saw videos of her wedding, she mourned the loss of her former self, as if a close friend or sister had died.

Kim was in such a depression that his boss said they should seek some counselling. This proved to be the turning point. Their therapist suggested they start from scratch and begin by dating again. Kim started taking Krickitt out for meals, bowling and sometimes he would bring her roses. She tried desperately to regain her former self, but as time went on she accepted herself for what she was *now*. Finally, it was she who suggested they should get married again.

Kim did not respond immediately – he wanted to be sure she really wanted him – then, on Valentine's Day 1996, he went to her office with a bunch of roses and proposed on bended knee. When he married Krickitt for the first time, he thought it was for life, and here he was again going through a new ceremony with a new wife.

HEAD TO HEAD

IDENTICAL twins Lavinia and Lorraine Christmas, who live in different Norfolk villages, decided simultaneously to visit one another on Christmas Eve 1994 to deliver their presents. They both set off at the same time and their cars met on a narrow, icy lane at Flitcham. The cars ran into one another and the thirty-one-year-old sisters were taken to the Queen Elizabeth Hospital at King's Lynn suffering from chest injuries, whiplash and concussion. As the twins' father was already in the hospital after a knee operation, Mrs Christmas decided she might as well have her Christmas lunch in the ward with the other Christmases.

Cases of coincidences between twins are well documented. A similar incident to the one above was inflicted on identical twins Frank and Jack Clatworthy. The pair went to a party and Frank left early. He was driving home to Washford, Somerset, when his car overturned. An hour later Jack, who knew nothing of his brother's misfortune, crashed on the same road. They finished up side by side in hospital.

Aaron and Liam Lynch are identical twins, and appear to be mirror images of each another. One is left handed and the other right handed. When one grazes the right knee, the other grazes his left. On Sunday 30 June 1995 Aaron broke his right collar bone when he fell off a fence. One hour later Liam broke his left collar bone when he slipped while out walking. At the hospital staff were astounded to see on the X-rays that the breaks were within 5 mm of each other.

In May 1996 identical twins William and John Bloomfield died just two minutes apart in Perth, Australia. A police spokesman said: 'They came into the world together and went out together.' Neighbour Ashley Williams told journalists: 'They did everything together. They'd take walks to the river or to the shops; it was always together. They were like an old married couple.'

They died from heart attacks while watching a body-building championship at a casino. Even in death they were inseparable. The authorities were experiencing difficulties in telling the twins apart. 'The coroner's office found a scar on one of their hips,' the police spokesman said. 'Then they found the other brother had an identical scar.'

The Meudelle twins, born in Paris, France in 1901, were found to possess the initials of their maternal grandparents on their shoulders in the form of birthmarks. The boy bore the initials 'TR' and was named Theodore Rodolphe, after his grandfather. His sister was christened Berthe Violette from the marks 'BV'.

There have been a number of studies carried out on identical (monozygotic) twins who have been raised separately with no contact between them. Some astounding coincidences have been recorded.

Twin boys born in August 1939 in Piqua, Ohio, were adopted by two families, the Lewises and the Springers, who were each told that the other twin was dead. They lived eighty miles apart and it was only six years later that Mrs Lewis learned by accident that the other twin was alive. While completing adoption papers, a clerk let the truth slip out when Mrs Lewis said she was calling her 'son' James. The clerk said she could not do that as the 'other little boy' was also called James.

It was not until February 1979 that James Lewis contacted his twin, James Springer, who was brought up believing his brother was dead. A startling number of coincidences had dogged their thirty-nine years. The two Jameses married and divorced Lindas and then married Betties. They had taken holidays on the same beach in St Petersburg, Florida. Both enjoyed carpentry and mechanical drawing, had police training and occasionally carried out police work. They both called their oldest sons James Allan. Relatives noticed similar speech patterns and posture. However, in one respect they were opposites: Lewis had short hair combed back and Springer had long hair combed forward.

DEATH DOUBLES

LABOURER Albert Steer left home in Bickley, South London in search of work one morning in May 1907. He told his family he was heading into Surrey, but the following day a man's drowned body was found by Chelsea Bridge. The description seemed to fit Albert Steer and, when his son and daughter visited the mortuary, they made a positive identification.

Their father had lost an eye – so had the dead man. One of his toes had been crushed; the body had a crushed toe too. Albert Steer's face was marked with a dent over one eyebrow where a piece of bone had been removed, and the corpse also had a dent.

The body was duly buried with a memorial stone on Bromley

Common. Two months later the family were shocked when Albert Steer returned home, explaining he had been helping a gardener at a house in Little Malden. The police, who still had a photograph of the dead man, now advertised for next of kin to come forward to identify a one-eyed, toe-crushed, head-dented man.

BLOOD BROTHERS

PARENTS try to treat their children equally, buying them new clothes at the same time, sweets, taking them out and giving them presents of comparable value. When Mr and Mrs Solf decided to buy their two sons a motorbike each, Fate decided to step in and keep up the time-honoured tradition. The boys were to learn that it was not only nice things that come in pairs.

In 1975 the boys left school and began work. Bodo was the oldest and the first to have a motorbike. He already had some experience of riding a friend's machine on a farm. Then Wolfy acquired his bike, practising along the country lanes around Honiton in Devon. When the accidents occurred Bodo had been riding his bike for two weeks and Wolfy for one.

On that day the boys went out separately in opposite directions. They left after Sunday lunch. Wolfy was the first to leave, unaware that Bodo also planned to go out. Mrs Solf's youngest went to visit a friend on the east side of town. As it was a nice sunny day they decided to ride over to Cotleigh, which was only a few miles away. They rode up a hill and hit a junction. But Wolfy only looked one way and carried on. To compound his mistake his engine stalled, and suddenly a car appeared which collided with him. Both his legs were injured, but his left leg was the worst. The impact sent the bones ripping through his jeans.

An ambulance arrived and Wolfy was loaded on board. It turned around and started travelling west towards the hospital in Exeter. After several miles the ambulance began to slow down, and Wolfy asked if they had arrived at the hospital. The driver said no, they were stopping to pick up another accident victim.

Wolfy watched as they stretchered a man into the vehicle: 'I recognised his two red boots. I asked them if they could assertain the other chap's name. It was Bodo. I told them it was my brother and they became excited. He just looked across at me and said; "Is it you, Wolfy?" And I said, "Yes. What's happened to you, Bodo?" He replied, "I've been knocked off my bike!" I said, "So have I . . ."'

Bodo did not know his brother had gone out when he decided to ride over to Bideford to visit his aunt and uncle. He had headed out of Exeter on the A30. Along the way he noticed a car up ahead parked in a bus lay-by. It was indicating to pull out, so Bodo slowed down. As he was virtually level with the car, it suddenly swung in front of him. Bodo swerved, but the car carried on and he hit the side of it. The impact sent him catapulting into the air to land in a heap fifty yards down the road.

A woman who had been trimming her hedge came out to help, and a lorry carrying soldiers stopped. Even though Bodo was having trouble breathing, he tried to stand up to see what had happened to his bike, which was trapped beneath the car. His attempt was short lived when his leg bent the wrong way. The soldiers made him lie down until the ambulance arrived.

He remembers vividly being wheeled inside: 'I was just lying there looking at the ceiling when I heard a voice saying, "Bodo, what are you doing here?" I thought I recognised that voice and I turned my head and there was my brother with an oxygen mask on his face. I remember the ambulance man shouting through to the driver, "We've got a right pair here – they're brothers!"'

Mr and Mrs Solf were still at home when there came a knock at the door. It was a police officer, who told them that their son Wolfy had been injured after a car had collided with his motorbike. As the officer was talking to the couple, the ambulance was being flagged down by people at the scene of Bodo's accident.

They rushed to Exeter hospital, thinking that Bodo was still on his way to Bideford. At the reception desk they identified themselves and asked to see their son. The receptionist asked which son they wanted to see as they had both of them there! A look of horror and disbelief passed across their faces.

The next twenty-four hours were the worst as both boys were operated on. When Mr and Mrs Solf went to the hospital next day, they found their sons recovering side by side in the same ward.

Afterwards, when Bodo told his father he was planning to buy a new motorbike, Mr Solf gave him his car instead. He said he thought it would be cheaper than paying for a funeral.

THE SMALLEST PART OF THEIR ANATOMY

TWO famous motorcyclists both suffered an identical injury and faced the same stark choice just hours apart. On 26 May 1980 Nigel Boocock, captain of Exeter speedway team and former English captain, badly damaged his little finger during a race. He was given the choice of amputation or of lengthy reconstruction of the digit. Boocock opted to have the finger removed so he could get back to training.

On the same day world famous-biker Barry Sheen was advised to have his own little finger amputated after an accident during the French Grand Prix at Le Castellet.

—·9·—
PLAGIARISED FROM REALITY

Authors use the word 'plagiarism' to describe the act of stealing another writer's words. There are examples, however, where writers have produced fiction which, it turns out, has been 'plagiarised' from real events that happen in the future. For example, student David Reynolds wrote an English essay in which he described being shot in the Hartford motel where he worked part-time as a night clerk. A few nights later he was gunned down by an unknown intruder. David had even got the time of his death right.

In the film *The China Syndrome* one of the characters remarks that a cloud of nuclear waste would wreak death and destruction over 'an area the size of Pennsylvania'. This was made before the nuclear accident at Three Mile Island. Better than this, a local magazine published a short story entitled 'Meltdown at Three Mile Island'. The author even got the date right – 28 March 1979.

Three weeks before the IRA murdered Lord Mountbatten on his yacht off the north-west coast of Ireland, a thriller by novelist Bill Granger was published entitled *The November Man*.

The plot concerned the IRA's plans to blow up the yacht of a British lord and cousin of the Queen.

German writer Ferdinand H. Grautoff wrote a novel in 1908 entitled *Banzai*. It described a future war between Japan and America. One of the characters was called 'General MacArthur'. In the story he led unprepared American troops against the Japanese – and was defeated. Almost four decades later the real General MacArthur rallied his men and defeated the Japanese.

Edgar Allan Poe was one of our finest horror writers. Fiction authors are often asked where they derive their ideas from. Science fiction author Isaac Asimov said he just 'plucked them out of thin air'. Many writers say they have no real idea where their inspiration comes from. Poe was a genius, but he was also an alcoholic, a drug addict and at times suffered from severe depression. Did this strange cocktail afford him a glimpse of the future or was it mere coincidence?

WILL THE REAL RICHARD PARKER STAND UP?

POE published his novel *The Narrative of Arthur Gordon Pym* in 1833. It told the story of a shipwreck, but centred around the plight of its survivors. Cast adrift in a lifeboat were several crew members and a cabin boy. Poe called the boy 'Richard Parker' and he was to be central to the plot in the novel and in real life. Faced with starvation, the other crew members in Poe's story decide to kill Parker and then eat his flesh. A graphic account is given of the victim's terrible fate.

Fifty years later the story became reality. *The Times* reported on 15 September 1884 that three men had been rescued from an open boat which had been launched from a sinking ship. On 31 October the newspaper produced more details. Apparently there had been a fourth survivor in the boat, a young cabin boy. The others had conspired to kill and eat him. His name was Richard Parker. . . .

The men were put on trial and convicted of murder. But, before they could be hung, there was such public outcry that their sentence was commuted to six months' imprisonment. They had cheated death not once, but twice.

There was another similar incident in the 1880s involving a playwright. Arthur Law wrote a play around the sole survivor of a shipwrecked vessel called the *Caroline*. The character's name was Robert Golding. A few days after the first performance Law read a newspaper account of a shipwreck and its sole survivor. The ship's name was the *Caroline* and the survivor, Robert Golding.

It was reported in 1977 that a Japanese container ship named the *Opan Bounty* was chartered to carry frozen foods from Australia to Iran. Captain David Blye was in charge of the vessel, and his first officer was William Fletcher Christian. Fortunately there was no mutiny on this *Bounty*.

WHAT'S IN A NAME?

AUTHOR Morgan Robertson had already written several novels set against the background of the sea, when he had a marvellous idea for another. In 1898 he penned a story entitled *The Wreck of the Titan*. It told how the *Titan*, an 'unsinkable' luxury liner, left Southampton in April for a trip across the Atlantic. Along the way it struck an iceberg and sank. An insufficient number of lifeboats resulted in the drowning of one third of the 3,000 crew and passengers.

In an edition of the magazine *Popular Mechanics* dated 7 April 1912 a short story appeared concerning another fictitious ocean-going liner, supposedly the largest in the world, which sinks after colliding with an iceberg near Newfoundland.

Fourteen years after Robertson's novel appeared, and a week after the magazine story, a ship left Southampton for New York. It was the maiden voyage of the luxury liner *Titanic*, a modern miracle of engineering, which the experts said was 'unsinkable'. Like the fictional *Titan*, it too had three propellers, was steel hulled and weighed 45,000 tons – just 1,000 tons short of the *Titan*. It, too, struck an iceberg and there was heavy loss of life owing to insufficient lifeboats.

A further twist in the tale involved a man born on the same day the *Titanic* sank. He was a crewman on board a ship called the *Titanian*, which set sail in 1935 for America. In the same area where the *Titanic* had sank, it too was struck by an iceberg, but did not sink. The outcome would have been much worse had the crewman not experienced a premonition of disaster and warned the navigator. He became more vigilant and steered the ship away from a head-on collision.

Finally . . . in 1980 a Bedfordshire family were at home watching a film called *Raise the Titanic!* when a huge chunk of ice fell out of a clear sky and smashed through their roof.

THE PRIME MINISTER'S BOAT IS MISSING

FORMER Prime Minister Edward Heath was at the centre of a bizarre and cruel coincidence on 4 September 1974. On

American Presidents Abraham Lincoln and John F. Kennedy are
linked by many strange coincidences as well as an assassin's bullet.
Above: John Wilkes Booth shoots Lincoln at the theatre.
Below: Kennedy discusses work with assistant Evelyn Lincoln.

In July 1900 King Umberto I of Italy (*above*) met his 'double',
a restaurant owner with whom he was to share the same fate. Film star
James Dean, seen below in *Giant*, died in his beloved red sports car – only
one of a gory train of disasters linked to the vehicle.

Not only manna falls from heaven – so too do a host of
strange objects including frogs and fish. In 1555 Olaus Magnus recorded
fish dropping from the sky (*above right*), while the fish below fell on
East Ham, London in May 1984.

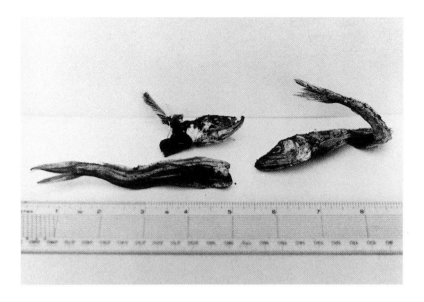

Absolutely flabuless

FED UP WITH TAUNTS, FAT FAMILY SHED 43 STONE

SIZE OF RELIEF: The scaled-down McNabs. From left: Dad, Leonard, Robert Jnr, mum and Heather

E cruel taunts of children made man-mountain Robert a loser in life now he couldn't be about it.

He and his 29st wife were tormented by of "There they are — two fun" as they strolled the street.

he end, they couldn't the insults — and decided some pounds simply had they switched to a strict diet and exercise plan.

results were amazing. McNabs and their three ildren shed 66lb — that's of flab between them.

ent, 53/10st 5st and now has less than he did when he His wife Jennifer, 35, got at 7lb from her 19st 11lb.

on Robert, 29, went lost 5st to 11st 7lb. Heather lost 65b to 9st 6lb and on, 28, from 17st 12lb to

the family decision to up, they all just ate o. Dad Robert would off 10,000 calories daily that was five fried eggs, five slices of buttered smeared with peanut and jelly, three doughn-d coffee with cream.

Fries

lay, the flabby five their way through cakes red ice cream, sand-crisps, hot dogs, biscuits ps. Lunch would be a s fast-food joint for two crepes each and serving s of fries

was a giant helping of token, slices of buttered bread.

Dad-Robert lost 16st

Mum Jennifer lost 7st Son Robert lost 5st

Daughter Heather lost 7st Son Leonard lost 3st

LIFE IN THE FAST LANE: The spot where Charlotte fell on to the busy motorway

Charlotte the fall girl makes a motorway exit

TODDLER Charlotte Donaldson is the luckiest girl alive after falling from a car as it drove down a busy motorway.

First her legs were dragged under the car and run over as she clung to the door sill at 30 miles an hour.

Then a tanker travelling behind narrowly missed the mischievous two-year-old.

But incredibly she suffered just a few cuts and bruises.

Her mother Dawn Norton said "Charlotte looks as if she had a little tumble off the bottom of a slide, not a fall out of a car accelerating on to a motorway.

"It could have been horrific but I think the Gods were with us."

Screamed

Charlotte had somehow man-

By ALUN REES

did cry for a few minutes but I think it was mainly shock. She must have undone the strap on her seat belt, opened the car door and stuck her leg out as it to get out of the car.

"Her legs got dragged under the car and she clung on to the

reading his comics as if nothing had happened." Father-of-two PC Peter Chew was the first offi-cer to arrive at the scene of the accident near Romsey, Hampshire.

"We had a call on the radio saying the baby had been run over and I feared the worst," he said.

"When we arrived we found a

FATHER TELLS HOW HE RESCUED SON L... IN A WATER-FILLED...

On the brink: Part of the McNulty family's Ford Escort in the water alongside the A47

Crash baby who was brought back from the dead

By SUZANNE O'SHEA

A FATHER whose car crashed into a water-filled dyke told yesterday of his desperate battle to save his baby son.

Having kicked his way out through the sun roof and ensured his wife and two older sons were safe, Sean McNulty realised there was no sign of ten-month-old Joshua, who had been strapped into his baby seat in the back.

"I thought at first that he was under the car seat but he wasn't," he said. "Then I got into the water, which was waist deep, but I couldn't see him."

The family from Silsden, near Keighley, West Yorkshire, were on their way home from a holiday in Caister, Norfolk, when the accident happened. Their luggage had spilled into the dyke.

"I kept on picking up items of clothing," said Mr McNulty, a 31-year-old landscape gardener. "I was going frantic because there were so many clothes in the water and everything looked like a baby.

"Then a woman on the bank shouted, 'He's behind you', and I saw Joshua's navy blue cardigan

Sean McNulty: First aid

Wife Anne: 'He's a hero'

with red spots floating in the water. I just pulled it out and he was there. His face was pale and his lips were going blue.

"I don't know what death looks like, but it looked as if he had already gone."

The trained first-aider began shaking his son and giving him heart massage as they lay on a grass verge beside the A47 at Acle, near Great Yarmouth. Another motorist involved in the accident,

31-year-old Alex Hardy, then began puffing tiny breaths of air into Joshua's lungs.

"This other man grabbed hold of him and stuck his fingers in his mouth to get the water out," recalled Mr McNulty.

"There was no response so I started slapping him on his back. I kept shouting that I was not going to let him die on me. I turned him over on his side and this stranger gave him mouth-to-mouth while I

Plucked from disaster: Joshua 'hardly has a mark'

did chest compressions. Suddenly he just sparked into life. He coughed and all this stuff came out of his mouth. When he started cry-ing I knew he was all right."

At that point shock, and the pain of his own injuries, overwhelmed him and he collapsed on the verge.

"I was lying there drifting in and out of consciousness, but I knew Joshua was all right because I could hear him crying in the dis-tance," he said.

Sitting up in bed cuddling Joshua he added: "I'm just so glad he is alive and well. It is so if he has come back from the dead."

Samantha Lee, 25, who was pass-ing the scene of Friday's accident with a friend, stopped to help.

The mother of two, who lives in Norwich, said: "It was just such a relief to hear the baby cry after the two men brought him back to life. After the father collapsed I just cuddled the baby in my arms."

Mr and Mrs McNulty were taken by ambulance to the James Paget Hospital, Gorleston with their sons Daniel, seven, and Andrew, five, but

Joshua went to Norwich Hospital, was reunited with Saturday.

They still have thrown out of a Ford Escort. "But a mark on him, 'only a couple head"

Mrs McNulty, absolutely distra accident because was missing.

"I remember screaming. 'My b baby is dead'. W crying I was over t all about the pain

"My husband is doubt that he sav Mrs McNulty, w such cuts and bruises from hospital to boys, who also had ries, left yesterday

Her husband w expected to have sur shoulder, which is badly gashed.

Murdered girl's body is found in ditch

By MICHAEL ORR and ROGER CLARKE

The naked body of a young woman was found in a ditch near the busy Chester Road, at Pype Hayes, Birmingham, last night, and detectives were working on the theory that the discovery could be connected with the disappearance of Barbara Forrest, a 20-year-old city social worker.

Mr. Maurice Buck, Assistant Chief Constable (Crime) in the West Midland Force, said at the scene: "This may be connected with the missing girl and it is being treated as murder.

The body was found within a few hundred yards of the children's home where Barbara Forrest worked as a child care officer.

Barbara has not been seen since the early hours of Bank Holiday Monday last week when she left her boyfriend in the Birmingham city centre to catch a bus after an evening out at a discotheque.

"After last night's discovery of the body, partially covered by bracken in a ditch only eight yards of the Chester Road, Det. Supt. Carol Lanahan, leading the search for Barbara immediately went to the scene to take charge of the new inquiries.

"The body was found at 6.15 p.m but was not moved until after 8.30 p.m when it was taken to the Newton Street mortuary, Birmingham, where a post mortem was carried out by a Home Office pathologist.

Mr. Buck added: "I have no information as to the cause of death and cannot identify the body except to say that it is that of a young woman.

"The police were expecting to be at the scene throughout the night. They had earlier collected items of clothing and

Barbara Forrest

know I was heading the same way. I was as far as I was fall.

"To put it simply, I was slick and tired of being slick and tired.

Under the double-diet his exercise steam from 45in to 30in, "the group TOPS — Take off Pounds Sensibly — some him International Loser of 1980.

The children were so impressed that they joined the pale in their quest for a healthy life.

Heather lost 280lb and husband Ken wanted children — not only now has she fallen pregnant.

 me Mary Ashford wh ed on the night of the tile. She attended a Whit liday dance at the Tyburn se Inn (below), and the morning discover him International social a young bricklayer.

ham Thornton (inset top). She left the dance in Thornton's company, and body was several times with him before her body was found next morning

8 MINUTE MIRACLE OF LAD ON BOTTOM OF CANAL

Lucky lad . . hero Bob Edward[s]

Tony vanishes underwater

Rescuer Bob revives him

[H]ero Bob saves 'dead' Tony

By MARTYN SHARPE

[A] BOY of nine survived [dr]owning after tumbling [int]o a canal — despite [ly]ing under water for [EI]GHT minutes.

[W]hen canal worker Bob [Ed]wards finally dragged in- Tony Wicks from the [mu]rky water he had no [he]artbeat or pulse.

[V]ictims who remain underwa[ter] for just four minutes nor[ma]lly die or suffer brain [dam]age.

[B]ut Bob, a qualified lifesaver, [gav]e Tony the kiss-of-life – and [a m]inute later he coughed and [ope]ned his eyes.

[A]n alarm call was registered [at] the canal office where Bob [wor]ks at 4.48pm. It was 4.56pm [whe]n Tony was dragged from [the] water and revived.

Coma

[D]octors believe Tony survived [bec]ause the shock of the cold [wat]er slowed his breathing and [he]artbeat to a near standstill. [It] left him in a coma-like [stat]e until he was brought round [by] Bob, 57.

[T]he lucky lad was in hospital [und]er observation last night, but [is] making a full recovery.

[N]on-swimmer Tony sank to [the] bottom of the canal in Don[cast]er, South Yorks, after he [slip]ped while playing on a jetty [wit]h cousin Joshua.

[Jo]shua, six, ran to the nearby canal office and told Bob – who immediately dived into the water. Bob said last night: "At first I simply couldn't find Tony in the water.

"It was only when I dived in feet first and felt his body with my toes that I realised he was there. He was lying on the bottom.

"I dived down again, grabbed his arm, and pulled him to the surface. I checked for signs of life but there was nothing.

"I thought he was dead. But I began mouth-to-mouth resuscitation and amazingly he coughed."

British waterways Inspector Bob, an ex-police superintendent, said: "He's incredibly lucky to be alive.

"I've been to see him in hospital, and told him he's got [to] start taking swimming lesson[s]."

Tony's mum Nadine, speaking [as] she sat by her son's hospi[tal] bed, said: "He must be [the] luckiest lad on earth. [An]d Bob's a real hero."

"He risked his ow[n life to] save Tony. I'll never [be able to] thank him enough."

Bob could be in li[ne for a] police bravery award. [A South] Yorkshire police spokes[man said:] "He undoubtedly save[d the boy's] life. Without his exper[tise it] would have been a tr[agedy."]

Relief . . mum Nadine yesterday

Trigger

Last night a medica[l expert] said: "It's a very unu[sual case] given that the boy wa[s under] water for eight minute[s.]

"In extreme cases, th[e functions] of the body suddenly [shut down when] immersed in water can [trigger a] defence mechanism.

"Vital functions, s[uch as] breathing and heart rat[e, slow] right down and appear t[o stop."]

● In April 1994 little [Karlee] Kosolofski was broug[ht back] to life after being frozen [in a] block of ice for six hou[rs out]side her home in [Rouleau,] Canada.

Karlee, two, had follow[ed her] dad Robert out of the ho[use on] his way to work in tempe[ratures] of -22°C at 2am.

Her mum found her at [break]fast time and rushed [her to] hospital where doctors ma[naged] to revive her even thoug[h her] body temperature had d[ropped] from a normal 98.6°F to

MY FORD FIASCO

DOUBLE Blundering Bill with his N-reg Fiesta – the car is identical to Alan's apart from its sun-[roof]

TROU[BLE]

By JOE ROBERTS

DOZY driver Bill . . .

KEEP-FIT FANATIC IN DEEP TROUBLE OVER RETURN TRIP RESCUE

Swimming saviour beats the lifeboat

Daily Mail Reporter

A KEEP-FIT fanatic swam through a gale to tell coastguards his friends were marooned in a stricken speedboat.

. . . up and Mr Alsop, a keen jet-skier, decided the only hope of rescue was to swim for it. 'The little boy was getting quite scared,' he said. 'I thought that . . .

Ignored warnings: Hospital . . .

ERIC'S

More gold is found on Roman site

[Er]ic . . . £10million find

EXCLUSIVE by KIERON SAUNDERS

[G]OLD strike pensioner Eric [La]wes was still coining it yes[ter]day after even more wealth [wa]s found on his treasure site.

[E]xperts scoured the area to [uné]arth well-preserved Roman [coi]ns worth up to £500 EACH. [T]he latest riches bear the head of [Rom]an emperor Honorius, who ruled [unti]l the year 423.

The coins were buried on the farmland near Hoxne, Suffolk, where Eric's metal detector pinpointed a chest of gold, silver and gems.

They lay yards from a stream named Gold Brook where workers found ancient coins 200 years ago.

Last night Eric's haul, which could be worth £10million, was under guard at the British Museum.

And the 70-year-old retired gardener revealed he could hardly see the loot as he unearthed it — because of cataracts. He is already blind in one eye and the sight is fading in the other.

Eric, of Denham, has waited eight months for surgery in Ipswich.

He said: "I have been expecting to hear from the hospital any day.

"They told me I should be able to see a lot better when the cataracts are removed.

"I certainly hope so. I really want to see all that treasure cleaned up and on display."

Eric vowed to keep on metal detecting when his sight is restored.

He added: "It's like fishing. You land a whopper but then you want to catch another."

Yesterday the museum showed off some of the haul including ornate spoons, bracelets, armbands and a solid silver tigress.

Roman Britain expert Catherine Johns said: "It obviously belonged to a very wealthy individual.

"Many of the items are solid gold or silver and in excellent condition."

"Twenty officials will spend a year on a report for a coroner's treasure trove inquest to decide how much Eric gets.

[Metal detector] man Mike Ridley tries out the Silver Saber 2

MOTHER ANSWERS PET'S YELPS AND FINDS TWO-YEAR-OLD UNDER THE WATER

Dog gives the bark of life as boy lies trapped in garden pond

A boy's best friend: Rhys cuddles up to German shepherd Henka yesterday in the garden where he nearly lost his life

A FAMILY dog tucked into extra helpings of his favourite Opal Fruits yesterday — for saving the life of two-year-old Rhys Loram.

Henka the German shepherd raised the alarm when the boy became trapped face down in a fish pond. The dog began barking furiously as Rhys fell through the pond's metal grid cover and ended up with his head and shoulders submerged.

When Rhys's mother Joanne rushed outside to investigate the commotion she found the animal desperately pawing at the little boy as he lay with his legs in the air.

Miss Louis, 29, scooped up her son and wept with relief when he opened his eyes and coughed up some water.

'There's no doubt in my mind that Henka saved Rhys's life,' she said. 'If he hadn't barked Rhys would have drowned.

'It would have been at least another 30 seconds before I had finished upstairs and gone to check on him. By then it would have been too late.'

The drama happened at bedtime for Rhys, the grandson of England speedway squad manager John Louis, and son of Miss Louis's boyfriend, Exeter speedway rider Mark Loram.

After his mother had dressed him in his favourite black and red Grand Prix pyjamas he insisted on one last game with Henka at their 16th century farmhouse in Stowmarket, Suffolk.

'I heard Henka barking and squealing in panic as if he was in pain,' said Miss Louis.

'I ran outside expecting to see the dog had hurt himself, only to see Rhys in the water. Henka was frantic and trying to dig him out.

'Henka is a very intelligent and loving dog. Rhys and Henka are inseparable. He instinctively knew that Rhys was in serious trouble and he had to get him out.'

Joanne: Heard barking

Rhys said: 'It was cold in the water and very dark. I thought the fish or monsters were going to get me, but Henka barked and mummy saved me.'

Miss Louis has decided to give away her 14 goldfish, drain the 18in-deep pond and turn it into a sandpit. She is getting used to her mischievous son's scrapes. Only three weeks ago she had to rescue him after he climbed up a ladder at the side of their house, which was being re-roofed.

Above: But for an unlikely sequence of events actor Anthony Hopkins might never have appeared in the 1974 film *The Girl From Petrovka*. Another amazing coincidence occurred after vital manuscript pages written by Camille Flammarion (*opposite below left*) were swept by the wind out of the study window at his home (*below*).

Conductor André Previn (*above*) made an astounding discovery during a chance visit to a bookshop in the Lubeck street below right.

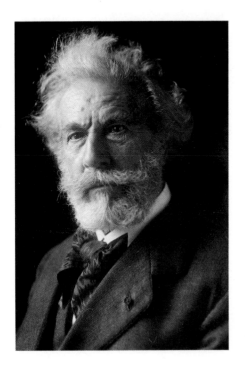

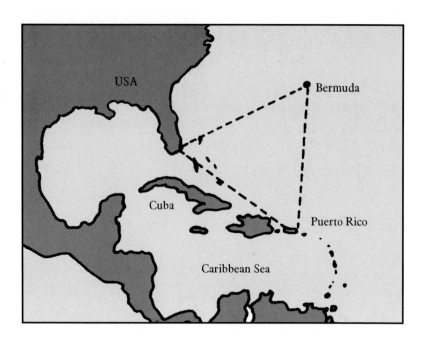

A sketch map showing the area of the Bermuda Triangle marked
by a broken line and (*below*) Avenger torpedo bombers of the same type as
those which vanished there.

that day his yacht *Morning Cloud* sank and two of the crew lost their lives. They had set sail on the morning of 1 September out of Burnham-on-Crouch, Essex, where they were competing in a week of racing. Mr Heath was not on board, and the yacht was skippered by the unfortunately named Donald Blewitt with an experienced crew of six.

By 11 pm they were out in the Channel and the weather had deteriorated to a force nine gale. Two of the men were washed overboard by a huge wave. One of them was hauled back, but the other was lost. As the boat manoeuvred to look for him, another freak wave hit the boat and Christopher Chadd, the Tory leader's godson, was then also washed overboard and drowned. The remaining crew took to the lifeboat and were picked up eight hours later.

Five days earlier Mr Heath had posed in a publicity photograph for a thriller written by John Dyson entitled *The Prime Minister's Boat is Missing*. The blurb ran: 'A blinding squall envelops a number of racing yachts in the English Channel; when it clears, the boat with the Prime Minister aboard has vanished . . .'

ROUND THE MOON

SCIENCE fiction writers often acquire a reputation for being able to predict the future. Usually this is because they are very skilful in extrapolating current ideas and trends into a futuristic setting. Sometimes, however, the events portrayed in S.F. mirror almost exactly future events.

One of the most popular and enduring early writers was Frenchman Jules Verne. Many of his novels have been filmed, including *Around the World in Eighty Days, A Journey to the Centre of the Earth* and *Twenty Thousand Leagues under the Sea*. But it was another of his stories, which predicted space flight, that came closer than one would expect to reality.

From the Earth to the Moon placed the launching of Verne's spacecraft in Florida, relatively near Cape Canaveral. The sequel, *Round the Moon*, came uncannily close to predicting the events surrounding an actual space mission – 100 years before its time.

Verne's spaceship, the *Columbiad*, took off for the moon, but an oxygen explosion prevented it from landing. In order to return the ship had to orbit around the far side of the moon, where gravitational forces acted like a sling and hurled it back to Earth. The bullet-shaped module landed in the Pacific, where the crew were rescued by ship.

The dramatic story of Apollo 13 was convincingly recreated in the film of the same name released in 1995. NASA were tempting providence when they called their third lunar lander *Columbia*. The ship took off at 13.13, but two days into the flight, on 13 April, a major problem developed. An oxygen tank exploded, curtailing the mission and putting the crew's lives in jeopardy. They were sent around the far side of the moon and catapulted back to Earth – just as Verne had predicted. The men were rescued after splash-down in the Pacific Ocean.

COINCIDENTAL DEATH OF THE
URBAN SPACEMAN

VIVIAN Stanshall, founder of the 1960s group the Bonzo Dog Doo-Dah Band, died in a fire at his north London flat on 5 March 1995 aged fifty-two.

One of the comic's creations was an archetypal English 'gentleman' called 'Sir Henry Rawlinson'. Stanshall used the character in his dialogue-free film made in 1980, *Sir Henry at Rawlinson End*, starring Trevor Howard. He later revived 'Sir Henry' for a series of radio sketches in the later 1980s recorded for the John Peel programme.

Did Stanshall realise that there was a real Sir Henry Rawlinson in the nineteenth century? He fought in many campaigns in India and was a celebrated Assyriologist. Sir Henry also deciphered the Persian cuneiform vowel system and was made a baronet. During his very active life he became President of the Royal Asiatic Society and of the Royal Geographical Society, as well as being MP for Reigate and Frome.

Sir Henry Rawlinson also died on 5 March – in 1895 – precisely 100 years before Vivian Stanshall.

IT SHOULDN'T HAPPEN TO A VET
(BUT IT DID)

BESTSELLING author James Herriot, whose semi-autobiographical books were serialised on television as *All Creatures Great and Small*, added another chapter in April 1994 when he was mauled by a pack of ewes. The seventy-seven-year-old vet – real name Alf Wight – was defending his flowers and vegetables in Thirsk, Yorkshire when the attack occurred. The biggest ewe caught the author on the garden path and sent him flying, breaking his leg. One of James Herriot's books is entitled *It Shouldn't Happen to a Vet*.

NETWORKED

MANY will remember the late Peter Finch in his Oscar-winning performance in the film *Network*. Finch played a newscaster by the name of Howard Beale, who threatens to commit suicide live on television before millions of viewers. The film actually had a real-life precedent, which occurred in 1974.

Christine Chubbock was a thirty-year-old television presenter responsible for a local news programme, *Sarasota Digest*, on Florida's Channel 40. It had just switched to a new format which had Chris reading the news and interviewing local personalities. Not long after the programme began technical difficulties ruined a clip of a shooting in a local bar. Apparently unperturbed, Ms Chubbock carried on: 'In keeping with Channel 40's policy of bringing you the latest news in living colour, you are going to see another first – attempted suicide.'

At this she produced a revolver from her lap, held it to the back of her head and fired. As she slumped forward thousands of viewers saw the screen black out. A company spokesman said Ms Chubbock had planned her suicide because they found on her desk an unofficial script which outlined her own death.

FAIRY TALES IN REVERSE

THERE are several stories reported in recent years from Eastern Europe that mirror fairy stories. Here are real-life versions of 'Little Red Riding Hood' and 'Goldilocks and the Three Bears'.

In 1970 six-year-old Elmira Godayatova went to visit her grandmother in a wood in Azerbaijan. After seeing granny, the little girl left for home but never arrived. A search was instigated which lasted over three weeks. Finally Elmira was found sitting beneath a tree, exhausted. She told rescuers that she had eaten berries, had drunk water from a spring and played with the 'wonderful doggies and puppies'. It became evident that she had been protected by wolves.

A similar story, also in Azerbaijan, was reported in various newspapers in 1978. This time a three-year-old girl named Mekhriban Ibragimov, who lived near the Caspian Sea, disappeared overnight while playing near a snow-filled ravine. Sixteen hours later she was found, sheltering in a cave with a wolf and her three cubs. Mekhriban explained: 'The big wolf licked my face. I snuggled up and she kept me warm. The little puppies cried.'

Five-year-old Goranka Cuculic became lost in a forest near the village of Vranje in former Yugoslavia one day in 1971. Her parents and other villagers combed the forest with torches. When woodcutters warned of seeing bears in the region, there was despair at ever finding little Goranka alive. Farmer Ivan Furian was, however, determined to find the child; armed only with a cudgel, he went on alone deep into the forest.

Ivan found the girl, at last, cold and hungry but unharmed. She told her parents and the other villagers how she had met three bears: 'One was big and fat, and the other two were quite small and cuddly. I played in a meadow with the two small ones, and shared my biscuits with them. The big one licked my face – its tongue tickled no end. At night I snuggled between the cubs and was beautifully warm.'

The following day she lost the bears and spent a night alone in the cave, cold and frightened. It was then that Ivan found her.

A modern day inversion of the fairy story 'Snow White and the Seven Dwarfs' came to light in 1979. Six-foot-tall, attractive blonde Nieves Boira had seven boyfriends. 'Nieves' is Spanish for 'snow', and the boyfriends were all below average height. Her neighbours sniggered when they saw the tall, beautiful girl in the company of her seven 'dwarfs'. But they smiled on the other side of their faces when Nieves suddenly became wealthy, driving a new car, wearing expensive clothes and visiting the top restaurants with her strange entourage of admirers. This happened at the same time as a number of jewellers were robbed – by seven men with sawn-off shotguns.

Nieves, it gradually transpired, had masterminded the robberies and had taken most of the proceeds. In return the men got their girl – until the law caught up with them and they were all thrown into jail.

THE JUNGLE BOOK

WHEN Rudyard Kipling created his character the man-cub 'Mowgli' in *The Jungle Book*, few readers and filmgoers realised that there has been a steady succession of real wild – or feral – children who have come to light over the centuries.

The first case was recorded in 1344, and up to 1961 fifty-three such children were discovered brought up variously by wolves, bears, leopards, panthers and gazelles. There were no new reports until twelve years later.

In 1973 a shepherd discovered a six-year-old boy living in a cave in the rugged Abruzzi mountains of central Italy. He walked on all fours and bit anyone who ventured near him. Attempts to trace his mother drew a blank. Doctors in a Milan hospital believe he was suckled by wolves, and attempts to place him with foster parents failed. Rocco, named after the rocky crag where he was found, was speechless and grunted in a 'half wolf, half goat' manner, and bit or clawed anyone who attempted to show him affection.

Two years earlier saw the discovery of a twelve-year-old boy in the southern jungles of Sri Lanka, living with a community of monkeys. The boy, named Tissa after the nearest village, could not speak, but barked and yelped, crawled on all fours and rested in a monkey-like posture.

French anthropologist Jean-Claude Armen excitedly reported his discovery of a boy living with a herd of gazelles thirty-five miles from Rio de Oro, as it was then known, the capital of the former Spanish Sahara. The long-haired naked youth was living like a gazelle and was mothered by one of the herd. Although he was observed walking upright, he was also capable of moving in leaps and bounds in imitation of his adopted companions. Mr Armen reported to the Life Institute in Geneva in January 1971 that he had watched him approach gazelles and lick their foreheads in a sign of recognition. He had also seen him dig for roots and feed them to his four-footed friends.

A real-life Tarzan was captured in 1968, living in the Mikumi Game Reserve in Tanzania. After escaping from previous attempts to capture him, rangers successfully swooped at dawn on the man's tree lair in the lion-infested reserve. They found him naked, whimpering like an animal, and unable to talk. He had apparently lived in harmony with the park's wild animals and had survived on berries and fruits. No one was able to identify him.

ANN QUINN'S FINAL CHAPTER

MYSTERY novelist Ann Quinn created a real mystery of her own in 1973. The thirty-seven-year-old author had written four books and several television plays, and, like one of her characters, was larger than life. She was described as being temperamental and excitable with a furious temper.

The final pages of her own life were written when a man fishing on Brighton beach saw Ms Quinn remove all her clothing and wade out to sea. Her body was discovered the following day two miles out in the Channel. Mr Mark Calvert Lee, Deputy Coroner at Shoreham, Sussex, told the inquest that there was no way of knowing whether she intended to commit suicide. He reported an open verdict.

METHOD ACTORS GO TOO FAR

ON 8 December 1971 opera star Marie Collier was killed in a way which mirrored her stage death. Five years previously she had stood in for Maria Callas in *Tosca* at Covent Garden, which was to be her last role before her death.

She was at home in the first-floor sitting room of her Panton Street house in London when, while talking to her financial advisor about a tour of America, she decided to open a window. She fell from the balcony thirty feet to her death. In the final act of *Tosca* the heroine leaps to her death. As an added twist, on the night that Marie died *Tosca* was once again playing at Covent Garden.

Actress Mary Ure was found dead by her husband Robert Shaw and their son on 3 April 1975. The tragedy occurred only hours after a triumphant first night in London's West End of a play in which she starred called *The Exorcism*. In a pre-publicity item the producer was reported as saying he was considering having the Comedy Theatre exorcised – just in case. After Ms Ure's death he publicly wished he had.

The play was about a woman possessed by the spirit of another, who had starved to death. Ms Ure's character is made to choke to death on her Christmas dinner. The celebrations which followed the performance found the leading lady on a high – yet not long afterwards she was dead. Mary Ure was believed to have choked on her own vomit.

− · 10 · −

FALLS FROM THE SKY

Ever since manna fell from heaven to sustain the starving Israelites there have been numerous stories of strange and unusual things dropping out of the sky. Phenomenalists call them 'fafrotskies' (falls from the sky).

Mrs J.P. Adams of Swindon, Wiltshire found a string of sausages caught in a tree during a storm, but one of the weirdest falls occurred in August 1708. Bishop Rhyzelius of Linkoping, Sweden wrote of the event in 1721 as part of his *Brontologia Theoligico-Historica*. According to his account, during a thunderstorm over Norrköping, a strange animal fell from the sky on to one of the streets. A number of eye-witnesses said the brownish creature looked like a beaver with a big lower jaw, a single small eye and short backbone. They thought it was a troll which had come down from the heavens! Researcher Anders Liljegren, who translated the text, was unable to discover what happened to the mystery corpse.

MORE MANNA FROM HEAVEN

ON St Patrick's Day 17 March 1992 Doug and Paula Ward of Bellington, Washington, were startled by 'a horrendous crash, like a sonic boom', followed by something crashing through their roof. It had all the appearance of twenty pounds of bread dough. A sample was taken away for analysis, which confirmed that it was indeed just ordinary dough. But how had it come to fall from the sky?

When a school was bombarded with eggs, was a hoaxer to blame or did they really fall from above?

The mysterious bombardment began in early December 1974 and stopped abruptly several days later. Parents taking their children to school at the aptly named Keep Hatch near Wokingham, Berkshire, ran for cover as the eggs rained down. They splattered on the playground, rooftops, fencing and cars. One witness, Mrs Ann Norman, said: 'They must drop from high up because they make a terrific noise when they hit the ground.' It was thought someone in a light aircraft might be dropping the eggs, but the Civil Aviation Authority did not think much of the idea.

In mid-1977 spates of egg falls occurred along West St Helen Street in Abingdon, Oxfordshire on Tuesdays and Thursdays over several months. James Heast of Glendale Electrical Services said that their premises had been hit around thirty-six times in five months. A woman standing outside an estate agents next door was hit on the head by an egg. Parked cars were egg smashed during the night. Shopkeepers who took turns to try and discover where the eggs were coming from gave up.

Some phenomenalists speculate that strange falls are the work of a planetary poltergeist – that the objects are actually teleported from their original location to re-materialise overhead. This next case might lend weight to such an idea!

Sometime in December 1975 Mrs Lynn Connolly of Hull was hanging out her washing when she felt a sudden sharp tap on the top of her head. A neighbour who heard her cry out came and helped Mrs Connolly search in the grass for the object which had caused the pain. They found a small silver note case, one and a half by two and a half inches, marked with some initials. It contained a half-used pad, on which was written the word 'Klaipeda'. This is the name of an old Lithuanian seaport.

Neither woman heard nor saw a plane overhead and, despite the publicity, no one claimed the case. As it only gave her a tap on the head, the conjecture must be that the object had only fallen a short distance.

A FISHY TALE

THERE are numerous accounts of fish falls. John Lewis was sawing wood at Mountain Ash in south Wales on 9 February 1859 when fish started falling all around him in the rain. There were hundreds of them, all alive, ranging from two to five inches long. They covered a strip of land 200 feet wide. It was thought they were indigenous to local rivers, although this did not explain the phenomenon.

The town of Rosewood in Queensland, Australia was visited by a fall of dead sardines at noon on 6 February 1989. It was initially witnessed by Harold Degen and his young son, returning home for lunch in the middle of a hail storm. Suddenly the hail turned to falling fish, and Harold persuaded his disbelieving wife to come outside. She said that the fish fell 'like silver rain', bouncing off the ground. They made a thick carpet across several square yards. The local bird population could not believe its luck.

Derek Gosling who lives in Sheerwater, Surrey, walked to the bottom of his garden early on 15 January 1993 and saw a fish on the path. When he looked around, he found others in the garden. They were on the lawn, in a rose bush, on his shed roof – all within a fifteen-foot radius. In all he counted a dozen fish, which were four to five inches long and looked like sprats – sea-water fish. His neighbour John Field also found eleven fish in his garden. The fish all smelled as if they had been out of water for some time.

Apparently the previous night there had been a storm with winds from the south-west. The nearest coastal water is forty miles away.

The aptly named William Fisher reported a mystery to the *Sunday Express* in January 1974. While he was visiting a trout farm near the village of Valls on the German-Dutch border, he found the workers puzzling over something. They were watching a salmon with a wound on its back swimming among the baby trout. Apparently it had not been there the day before and, as usual, the farm had been guarded during the night. They speculated that a large bird such as an osprey had caught the salmon at sea and dropped it in the pool. However, the coast is more than 100 miles away, so how could a bird have carried it all that distance, and how had the fish survived so long out of water?

PEAING CRABS

AFTER a tremendous storm over Swansea in September 1981, Mr Cliff Davies of Killay found two crabs in his garden. One was badly mangled, but the other was very much alive, so he released it in the sea five miles away.

Elsewhere in Wales at the beginning of April 1980 Mr Trevor Williams of Tonna, Glamorgan thought the hard objects hitting the surface of his pool were hailstones. He was in his garden when the shower began and it soon became obvious that something very odd was happening. 'I couldn't believe my eyes,' he said, 'I expected hailstones, but there were peas everywhere. They were bouncing off the greenhouse and house roof in their thousands. The storm lasted several minutes and I was able to collect several jam-jars full of peas.'

RAINING FROGS

FROG falls are often reported by first-hand witnesses. John Pitman, his wife Caroline and their two children were travelling by bus in August 1944 from Birmingham to the village of Hopwas, near Tamworth. It was late morning when they were walking past Whittington Barracks. The weather was hot and the sky blue except for several heavy cumulus clouds that had made the morning showery. Suddenly it began raining again and the family ran for cover beneath a tree.

As Mr Pitman explained: 'We were caught in a shower of rain which also contained many hundreds of frogs. I guess they were approximately fifteen millimetres overall. Prior to the heavy shower the road was completely clear. Whilst I cannot say I actually saw frogs fall, the road and path became covered with living frogs, whereas the dry area under the tree remained clear. As it was a hot day, soon after the rain stopped the road dried quickly, leaving the gutters still flowing with water. The frogs jumped into the gutters and any puddles that were left.'

Mr Pitman speculated that the frogs had been caught up in a

current of air from a field which ran by the River Tame. Approximately ten years later a Mrs Mowday and her son had a similar experience in nearby Sutton Coldfield.

They were in Sutton Park to see a Royal Navy display in June 1954. The weather conditions were similar in that there were frequent heavy showers. After visiting all the major exhibits they decided to take a quick look at the fair. Suddenly it began raining, so they sought shelter beneath some trees on the fringe of the park.

'We were bombarded by tiny frogs which seemed to come down with the rain. There were literally thousands of them. They descended on our umbrellas, on us and we were afraid to walk for fear of treading on them.'

Mrs Mowday found that whenever she or her son related the experience to anyone they received 'incredulous disbelieving looks'.

A letter appeared in *TV Times* for 12 February 1960 from Grace Wright of Hounslow, Middlesex. She described how, fifty years before, she had been walking along a street in the town with her husband and small son when a heavy storm broke. At first they thought the tiny missiles that fell were hailstones, but it soon became apparent they were in fact tiny frogs. These frogs were very much alive. Her son filled a sweet box to take home, and Mr Wright managed to collect a large number in his hat. There were still very many more left in the street.

Sunday Express columnist Veronica Papworth shared a frog fall incident with *Fortean Times* magazine editor, Bob Rickard. She told him it happened in 1969, when she was living on a high ridge in Penn, Buckinghamshire. It had been a hot, stormy, summer evening with the threat of rain in the air and heavy black clouds overhead. Suddenly the storm broke and, when she and her husband looked out on to the patio, there were hundreds of tiny black frogs jumping in the rain. They watched the downpour for several minutes as more frogs appeared on the patio and the lawn beyond. Unfortunately they had to go out and by the time they returned home the frogs had all vanished.

Frog falls, although rare, are not as uncommon as many people think. When one case is reported, it inspires many other witnesses to do the same. The following appeared in such circumstances in the *Camden News* in Arkansas:

> In the summer of 1926 I caddied at a local golf course. There had been a long drought that summer and the fairways were brown and dried up. One afternoon, a sudden storm came up and a terrific thunder shower followed. Rain came down in torrents, and with it a shower of tiny frogs about the size of nickels. They were alive and jumping – thousands of them. The golfers and I couldn't believe our eyes as we watched thousands of frogs come right down with the rain from the sky.

Falls of fish and frogs during a storm are often thought to have been sucked out of ponds, rivers or the sea by whirlwinds or waterspouts and then later deposited. One wonders, however, how these creatures could possibly survive such a transition? Phenomenalists also question how such natural phenomena manage selectively to scoop up creatures and objects of *only one kind?* However, one account that appears to back the whirlwind theory was published by the *Journal of Meteorology* in October 1986. It was vividly described by J.W. Roberts of Kettering, Northamptonshire, who, in 1919, was working on a farm during his school holidays.

> I was walking between the stacks of hay and straw when there was a sudden rush of air. I looked up towards a disused quarry cutting and saw a dark, almost black cloud rushing

towards me. It was a whirlwind. It picked up some of the loose straw lying about, and when it reached the buildings it seemed to stop. The dark cloud suddenly fell down and I was smothered all over with small frogs – thousands of them about one and a quarter to one and a half inches long. I think they must have come from a lake a mile away up from the cutting. Oh boy, was I scared. I ran across the footbridge over the brook right close to our house, and my mother could hardly believe me, only I had small frogs in my shirt.

Critics believe that in many cases frogs have been hiding in undergrowth, and a sudden downpour brings them out, giving the impression they have fallen with the rain. The beginning of this next account sounds as though this could be the explanation, but then comes the twist in the tale . . .

Mrs Vida McWilliam told *Fortean Times* magazine of the shock she received after a wet and windy Sunday in June 1979. The following day it was very damp and humid. She went outside and on the patio noticed hundreds of half-grown tadpoles and many more tiny frogs. Mrs McWilliam said to her family, 'It must have rained frogs on Sunday.'

Later in the week she went down the garden to cut the lawn and found the grass covered with green and black frogs. But, more importantly, she also found frogspawn hanging from the bushes, proving that the creatures had indeed arrived with the storm.

BLOBBY, BLOBBY, BLOBBY . . .

HURRICANE Andrew deposited something blobby in Elwood Guillot's pond near Louisiana. The blobs were discovered on 26 August 1992 when Elwood's grandson, Michael Guillot, was inspecting the storm damage. He fished a number of the things out of the pond. The largest was over a foot across, and it was not clear whether the blobs were animal, vegetable or chemical. A biologist Bob Thomas, who examined them, was of the opinion that they were 'harmless crowds of single-cell organisms'.

The magazine *Fortean Times* also reported that a similar blob, still alive, was found on the north shore of Rondeau Bay, Shrewbury, Ontario. Nick Glazier, owner of a duck-hunting lodge, spotted it floating in a pond. When he tried to catch it in a net, the blob swam under water and disappeared. A week later they had better luck and captured it. A man from the Ministry of Natural Resources examined it and made a vague comment to the effect that it 'may' have come from the 'tropics'.

That was not the first time something blobby had been recorded in Ontario. On the afternoon of 16 June 1979 Donna Matchet was raking leaves from the family swimming pool in Mississauga when a crash alerted her. Donna turned around and saw a gooey green mess on a picnic table close by. A flame was coming from it like a jet from a blowlamp. She quickly extinguished it with a hosepipe and called her parents.

The mass solidified into a flat object weighing a few ounces. It was examined by the Ministry of the Environment, who concluded it was a type of plastic commonly used to make toys. It had been heated, melted and resolidified. They speculated that a flare had struck a child's frisbee and set it on fire, whereupon it had landed near the Matchets' swimming pool.

A report by the police forensic science laboratory in Toronto came up with broadly the same conclusions, but added that, due to combustion, no precise identification was possible. The Matchets tried to duplicate the effect suggested by the experts by trying to set a frisbee alight with a blow torch. It took several minutes to light and then it only smouldered. It later emerged that three other blobs of the plastic material had fallen in the area over the previous few months. One at Brampton was three times the size of the Mississauga object.

A green slime fell all over the Foggy Bottom area of Washington during 5 and 6 September 1978. It dotted gardens, and pets who had presumably eaten grass coated with the goo became sick. Tests by the Bureau of Occupational and Institutional Hygiene failed to identify it. However, they did eliminate the slime being aviation fuel or pesticide. The principal elements were nickel sulphate, iron sulphate and manganese. They said it was highly acidic and the product of combustion – although it had definitely not come from an aircraft.

Firemen were called out shortly after midnight on 10 July 1978 to put out a small blaze at the junction of Third Street and High School Avenue, Council Bluffs, Nebraska. At the centre of the fire in an impact crater they found a mass of molten metal measuring three feet across by three inches thick. Five days earlier a similar blob hit the junction of McGee Avenue and Harrison Street which took thirty minutes to cool down. Details of any analysis were not reported.

ON THE ROCKS

THERE are many accounts of ice falling out of the sky. Researcher Ronald Willis recorded forty-six falls between 1802 and 1968. This includes a monstrous mass of ice nearly twenty feet in circumference and of proportionate thickness that fell at Ord, Scotland in 1849. Some people speculate that they are from outer space, debris from passing comets – although how ice would survive the fierce heat of speeding through the atmosphere is not known. The modern explanation is that they are pieces which have fallen off the wings of aircraft or are the contents of loos jettisoned during flight. 'Coincidentally' on 7 March 1983 a block of ice about a foot thick crashed through the roof of a warehouse belonging to Alltransport International – near Birmingham Airport. Were aircraft to blame for the following fall?

A six-pound ball of ice smashed through the roof of a bungalow in Barnsley, Yorkshire in September 1973. The house belonged to an old lady and her grandson, thirteen-year-old 'T. Upton', provided researcher Phil Ledger with some details.

Apparently the phenomenon struck at three in the afternoon on the day of the Finningly Air Show. Barnsley is beneath the flight path used by many European aircraft heading for Manchester Airport. Apart from the ball, fragments as big as a hand were found scattered in the gardens of other houses. No one saw or heard the ice falling even though it was a bright sunny day. When it melted, the water looked dirty.

This next case makes one wonder if aircraft explanations hold water.

Fifty-eight-year-old Eric Cooper was walking his dog on a private road at Lonkill Farm, near Thorpe Constantine, Staffordshire on 19 December 1975 when he saw something flash by and break up on impact. The main chunk embedded itself one foot deep in the hard ground just yards from where he was walking. He went over to examine it and saw it was part of a circular disc of ice about six feet in diameter, weighing some 6lb. The Civil Aviation Authority thought it was unlikely to have fallen off a plane, but could be attributed to 'a weather phenomenon'.

Wilbert Cullers and two friends in Timberville, Virginia received a shock on the night of 7 March 1976 while they were watching television. At 8.45 pm they were startled by a crash which shook the house. A lump of ice 'about the size of a basketball' tore through the metal roof tiles, sheared a roof strut and made two large holes in the plasterboard ceiling.

About an hour later deputies from Rockingham County Sheriff's Department arrived and collected three buckets of the ice, which Sgt Hottinger described as 'milky white and compressable in the hand'. A neighbour standing in his drive had heard the impact, which sounded 'like a muffled shotgun', then about twenty seconds later had seen another object hit the road some fifty yards distant. A young girl living opposite rushed out when she heard the impact with Cullers' roof and also saw the second block hit. The temperature was around 35°C at the time. Later a third block of ice was found about a mile away by a farmer feeding his chickens.

None of the witnesses saw or heard an aircraft in the clear sky. Tests carried out on the ice were inconclusive. This case, however, highlighted another explanation often touted for ice falls – that the debris is from a passing comet. Dr Charles Tolbert of the University of Virginia stated that, in his opinion, the ice at Timberville could not have come from a comet.

A block of ice measuring three foot by eight inches smashed through the roof of 402 High Street, Ponder's End, Enfield at 8.20 pm on 2 January 1977. Chronic bronchitis sufferer James Pluck was just about to return to his sickbed when the block smashed through the bedroom ceiling, hurling plaster, slates and jagged fragments of ice all over the bedroom. Mrs Clara Pluck thought there had been a gas explosion. If her husband had been in bed, he would have suffered injury or worse. Pieces of the stuff could still be seen on their lawn two days later.

Eye witnesses in Pinner, Middlesex had a narrow escape on 25 March 1974 when a cube of ice measuring eighteen inches square smashed roof tiles and stove in the bonnet of a car. Mrs Doris Fox was gardening just after 5 pm when she saw 'a huge white ball which looked as if it was making straight for me'. She ducked as it went over making a noise like a firework rocket. A loud crash followed as it hit her nextdoor neighbour's car.

The car belonged to Mrs N. Wildsmith, who was cleaning it at the time. She was just a couple of feet away when the ice bomb struck. Mr Albert Fox, who was also in the garden, looked up on hearing the collision and, seeing ice all over the car, thought that the Wildsmiths' refrigerator had exploded through the front window. It was also witnessed by a Ms Elsie Urquhart, who lived in the next road.

A bucket full of the yellowy-brown ice was preserved for analysis, but there is no record of what became of it. The Civil Aviation Authority were of the opinion that it was waste water released from an aircraft. Waste tanks are normally emptied on the ground. One would have thought that the chemicals in any effluent would have prevented it turning into ice.

The next incident contains an odd detail. Farm labourers working in a field at Abbeville, France on 11 March 1978 were startled by a loud explosion – followed by a whizzing sound like an artillery shell. They found a fresh crater in the ground which contained a twenty-five kilo lump of transparent ice with a greenish tinge.

Finally, here is a one-in-a-million ice fall coupled with a coincidence – a ball of ice that fell at the feet of a meteorologist!

Dr Richard Griffiths was out walking in Didsbury, Manchester during a storm on 2 April 1973. He was at the junction of Buttesford Avenue and Burton Road when 'a large object struck the road about three metres to my left. The object fell fast enough to shatter into many pieces on impact.' The largest piece weighed just under 1½lb and was preserved for analysis.

The original shape was similar to a rugby ball. It was composed of rings of ice – like the layers of a tree – in which were trapped bubbles of air. The object fell nine minutes after a single flash of lightning covered the whole of the Manchester area. That came during a day of gales, heavy rain and even a light snowfall in the morning.

Aircraft were ruled out and Dr Griffiths concluded that the ice had not formed in a container: 'The sample displays a puzzling collection of features. While it is clearly composed of ice-water, there is no conclusive evidence enabling one to decide precisely how it grew. In some respects it is like a hailstone, in others it is not.'

The main problem which confronted the meteorologist was how an object of such size could remain in the sky long enough to form.

NUTS, BEANS AND HAY

Mr and Mrs Wilson-Osborne were walking home from church on 13 March 1977 when a dark cloud appeared and loomed overhead. They were outside the White Tree Garage in Bristol when it began to rain – nuts.

Mr Wilson-Osborne described the phenomenon: 'At first I thought it was a heavy hailstorm, but no, they were hazelnuts. They were peppering down on the road and bouncing off cars. They were coming from the sky, from what I would estimate as a considerable height. I collected half a dozen or so to take home. I tried one of the nuts and it was sweet, fresh and quite delicious.'

When they arrived home, a neighbour called to say that he, too, had been showered with hazelnuts!

Brazilian farmer Salvador Targino was showered with beans on 1 June 1971. There was no storm at the time and the beans were identified as African. Officials speculated that they had been scooped up by a storm in Africa and carried across the ocean before being dumped on Brazil.

On 22 July 1976 it rained straw outside the Barclay Arms, Bosham in Hampshire. One of the witnesses, Mrs Valerie Cresswell, said: 'It came down from a cloud that was passing over. Luckily one of the guests saw it as well because I thought I was going barmy.'

The Meteorological Office in Southampton suggested that a tornado could have been to blame. That same day straw also fell over the city of Lincoln, festooning buildings, roads and telegraph poles over a wide area. Witness Peter Twartz said that the hay was coming down in such quantities it was as if an aircraft was dropping bales. Another man told reporters that the 'sky was full of straw, and people were walking around with armfuls of it'. A light aircraft pilot reported seeing the equivalent of whole hay stacks at high altitude.

Five days later straw dropped on Scunthorpe, twenty miles north of Lincoln. If it was part of the same shower, how did it manage to stay up in the atmosphere all that time?

On 8 August 1977 in Poole, Dorset holidaymaker John Kay noticed it was raining. Suddenly it stopped raining, then began again – this time with hay and clumps of grass with soil still attached to the roots.

A STONE'S THROW

ARE reports of stones appearing from the sky further indication that some falls at least are the work of 'poltergeist energies'?

A hail of stones bombarded a garage in Aversa, southern Italy in 1980. The barrage was so violent that it frightened the manager, Nicola Grassia and his twelve-year-old son, Enzo. During the 'attack', Grassia flagged down a passing police car and the officers stepped out into a hail of stones. One shattered a window in the vehicle and another dented the bodywork. Thinking someone was hurling the stones, the officers fired warning bursts into the air from their machine-guns. But the nearest building was twenty-five yards away and a search for culprits drew a blank.

In the poltergeist literature there are records of stones apparently materialising in buildings. Objects that arrive in this way are called 'apports'. This next account indicates that some falls might be apports.

South African tennis players Okkie Kellerman and Andre Wulfse, both aged seventeen, were travelling to Maritzburg for the Natal Open Tennis Championships in July 1980. The train temporarily pulled into a siding when they reached the city, and on the platform stood a strange-looking man wearing a safari suit and carrying what looked like a doctor's bag. As Okkie was suffering from a cold, he pulled down the window and jokingly asked the man if he was a doctor. The stranger replied that he was, in fact, a witchdoctor. The young men laughed. Their impression of a witchdoctor was someone wearing tribal clothes, not smart western dress. Laughing, Okkie asked him if he had a cure for a cold. He told Okkie to use some Vick.

They laughed again as the train pulled out, and it was obvious that the witchdoctor was upset by their attitude. As they disappeared down the tracks he stood wagging his finger at them. Was it coincidence that the following day they were besieged with stones raining down on them?

After a practice lesson a stone suddenly landed on Okkie's

shoe. Naturally he thought he had kicked it up, but further down the road a bigger stone fell out of the air and landed next to him. He ducked behind a wall thinking someone was using him for target practice. As he crouched, Okkie could hear stones falling all around him in nearby bushes. When the barrage ceased, he ran the rest of the way to his lodgings. But it was not over. Every time he or Andre tried to leave the house 'suddenly the stones would be all around us'.

Even indoors they were not safe. On the evening of 11 July Okkie was woken up by a stone dropping off his bed on to the floor. Andre was asleep in the same room. Then stones began to pelt Okkie. He awoke Andre and they collected the stones, and put them on the dressing table. Okkie put a pillow over his head and tried to get back to sleep, but the stones kept coming. After three hours the youths were scared witless and awoke their land-lord, Peter Dove. They spent the rest of the night in his room. He later confirmed that the boys were genuinely afraid and saw the stones for himself. After they left the house the stones stopped falling.

IT'S ALL BALLS

HAVE showers of golf balls fallen from the sky? A police investigation failed to account for a shower of golf balls which arrived during a storm at Punta Gorda in Florida. In a letter to the magazine *Fortean Times* Mr A.T. Ryland of Sandersfoot, Dyfed told of his strange discovery in April 1975.

He was out tracing a disused footpath a mile west of the pretty seaside town across rough, unfrequented ground. He noticed a golf ball in the grass and then, upon looking around, found about a dozen. He thought at first they must have been lost by 'a careless and affluent golfer' who was out practising, but realised that no golfer with any sense would play in such a wild area. The nearest club was over three miles away.

Mr Ryland returned a few days later and made a more thorough search. Altogether he found a total of thirty golf balls in an area of fifty by thirty yards. Many of them had been trampled into the ground by cows, and he speculated that there were probably more balls to be recovered if he were prepared to dig. Their condition varied from pristine, clean-looking balls to some that were badly battered.

He wondered if seagulls had transported them there and wrote to the Royal Society for the Protection of Birds. They thought it unlikely.

Mr Ryland continued to visit the site for the remainder of 1975, but found no more balls. During the beginning of the following year the ground was so muddy it was not practical to continue his search. However in April, a year after the initial discovery, Mr Ryland once again collected around thirty balls. How had they arrived there?

Employees at a waterworks in Sutton, Surrey were confronted by a mystery in July 1981. Over several weeks golf balls had been accumulating in the grounds. On separate occasions two men had narrowly escaped being hit by balls. There was not a golf course for miles around, so where had they come from? It was suggested that they were being hit from a nearby garden, but there was never any evidence. Had they 'fallen' from the sky?

Although well documented, falls of strange objects are rare. However, next time it rains it might be a good idea to wear a hard hat in addition to carrying an umbrella!

— · 11 · —
OBJECTS OF COINCIDENCE

Inanimate objects often play a strong role in the realms of coincidence and those special one-off events. It is tempting to believe that soulless machines created by man can take on a life of their own or are temporarily manipulated by an outside force as in a plot of a Stephen King novel.

Early in the morning of Friday 29 March 1974 the train at Caterham, Surrey was prepared as usual for departure to central London. When the pre-run tests were complete, the driver and his guard went for a cup of tea. At 6.34 am the train pulled out of the station with no passengers and no driver. . . .

For nine miles it ran at speeds of up to forty miles per hour. Attempts by British Rail staff to divert or stop the train met with failure. It hurtled through seven stations before being directed into a buffered siding at Norwood Junction.

None of the main drive motors had been switched on, but the route was mostly on a downward gradient. However, this does not explain how the air brakes and the dead man's handle were circumvented to allow the train to run. An official investigation was subsequently held – behind closed doors.

Coincidences seem to occur around those involved in reporting coincidences. While Peter Hough was writing the above, he was astonished to hear a train whistle outside his house even though the nearest line is several miles away! Upon investigation, he discovered that the sound had come from a steam engine driven along the road by Fred Dibnah. The massive machine was making its laborious journey to Warrington to take part in a steam fair.

DOUBLE TRACK

Is there a connection between two train derailments fifty-six years apart? On 9 October 1995 an American train was sabotaged in Hyder, Arizona, killing one of the crew and injuring over 100 passengers. During their investigation, the FBI uncovered similarities with a disaster that occurred in Nevada, Texas on 12 August 1939 in which twenty-four people died.

Both trains were westward bound, travelling at night through desert on track owned by Southern Pacific Railroad. Both were derailed at the end of a bridge when they were diverted into a stream bed. This was done through tricking the signalling system by shorting out the two split rail ends. In both cases the inside spikes were pulled from eleven ties. Photographs of the crashes were indistinguishable from one another.

Letters found at the scene of the Hyder crash were signed 'Sons of Gestapo' and contained a diatribe against the sieges at Waco and Ruby Ridge. The FBI thought these were a red herring, although during investigation of the Nevada derailment suspicion was cast on Nazi sympathisers.

Investigators found that two weeks before the latest crash a railway magazine entitled the *Southern Pacific Tramline*, produced in Dunsmuir, California, printed a detailed account of the 1939 disaster. The FBI concentrated their attentions on disgruntled ex-employees of the rail operator, Amtrak, who planned to close part of the Southern Pacific line with heavy redundancies.

Despite this promising line of enquiry, the FBI have no firm leads, no witnesses and no suspects. In both cases no one was ever arrested.

HOMEWARD BOUND

PAUL Besford shares a house with two other men in Norwich. In November 1995 one of the other men bought an Austin Allegro. It was a good little runner, and Paul bought it off him one month later. When its MOT was due, he sold it to someone else.

A week later he was in the back garden tidying up the borders and was about to start work in the front. Suddenly there was the sound of crunching metal and smashing glass. Paul thought a motorcyclist had come off his bike and rushed round to the front of the house. There he could not believe his eyes.

A car had come storming over the hill and through his garden fence, cleared a wall and embedded itself in the front of the building. A concrete pillar saved the house from destruction, although the upper window had shattered just missing one of Paul's friends who was in the room.

The car was the Allegro that Paul had sold the week before. Apparently two girls had taken it without permission and the driver had lost control. The girls escaped with whiplash, cuts and bruises.

CAR CONFUSION

A TALE of two Ford Fiestas resulted in one driver being chased by police. Bill Ives parked his red N-registered car next to Alan Burch's K-registered model of the same colour. After visiting relatives, Bill went over to Alan's car and drove off in it using his key.

When Alan discovered his car had gone, he immediately reported it as stolen. Police in Marlborough, Wiltshire spotted Bill driving it and gave chase. A posse of police, including several cars and a helicopter, stopped Bill on the A4. He still thought it was his own vehicle and argued with officers PC Alfie Ansell and WPC Burns until they showed him the number plate.

Bill demonstrated how his key fitted Alan's car door and ignition, but Alan's key, while it would lock Bill's door, would not unlock it or turn the ignition. Ford described the mix-up as a two-billion-to-one chance.

Marie Eads Ries of San Pablo, California was involved in a similar mix-up in the 1930s. At that time she lived near Coalinga and her husband bought her a new Ford two-door from a dealer in Fresno.

She told *Fate* magazine in June 1986: 'I had had the car about a week when I drove into Coalinga and parked on a main street. I shopped, came out of the store, unlocked my car and started to back out. I saw a strange hat and briefcase on the back seat just as a man rushed into the street, yelling: "Come back with my car!"'

Her car was parked next to the one she had unlocked. She had not even noticed that another car, same model, make and colour, was parked next to hers. Apparently the owner of the other car had bought it ten days earlier in San Francisco – 300 miles away.

The author of this book, Peter Hough, was involved in a mix-up involving two grey Mini vans. Hough had taken his girlfriend to a country pub one evening and, when they came out, it was dark and raining. He went over to where his vehicle was parked and unlocked it; his girlfriend settled in beside him. It was only when she noticed that the wing mirror was a different design that he realised they were in the wrong vehicle – yet it was the only Mini van on the car park.

At first they thought the owner of the van they were in had accidentally driven off in Hough's vehicle, as they had apparently been parked next to one another. Unfortunately it transpired that his Mini van had been stolen.

SUMMER HOLIDAY

SOMETIMES people feel controlled by destiny. No matter what obtacles get in their way they still reach their goal. Was it destiny that ensured a blue Ford Sierra went on holiday to France with its former owners? How did the car, which was towed to a scrap yard after an accident, 'rise from the dead'?

Sue and Brian Luck had never had a decent car before, just a series of old bangers. Now they could afford something better and were keeping an eye out for a suitable vehicle. Brian wanted something sporty, while Sue was on the look out for a family saloon. They had been searching for some time and were on their way to Weston-super-Mare when they saw a little garage at Uphill.

On a whim they pulled in to see what was on offer. There were two cars that they each instantly fell in love with. One was a sporty-looking Peugeot and the other a blue Sierra. The Ford immediately attracted Sue. She knew it would be exactly right. Brian, however, could see himself behind the wheel of the Peugeot.

They had a look at both the cars, but Brian had his heart set on one and Sue on the other. The pair left the garage and argued about it for a day or so. Finally they decided to return to the garage and test drive both vehicles, but, when they arrived, they discovered the Peugeot had been sold. Brian was disappointed, but Sue had been working on him and, when they sat in the Sierra, both of them felt *right*.

Brian explained: 'It wasn't the car I was looking for. But once I'd driven it, you know, *once driven forever smitten*. It was a very nice car with a low mileage – and that suited us just fine.'

Sue added: 'It was big and roomy, a really nice, comfy car. I can't really explain it, I just liked it and thought, *yes, we're having this car*. It just seemed to drive itself. In any case we needed a decent car to go on holiday – the Sierra seemed to fit.'

Brian found himself looking after the Sierra as he had never cared for any previous car. As soon as they reached home he was waxing the bodywork and showing it off to friends and colleagues at work. The vehicle filled him with pride. A few months later they were making plans for their annual summer holiday. They usually went away with Sue's sister, Trish, and her husband, Ray. Although they had never motored abroad before, the car filled them with confidence and Sue picked up some brochures about camping in France.

It had always been Brian's ambition to go abroad with his own car, and now the blue Sierra would make that possible. After spending hours searching through the glossy brochures, they found a camp that suited them. There was a club and entertainment for the couples' children. They booked the holiday twelve months in advance because Sue always liked to be sure.

They looked forward to the break and settled back to wait for the time to arrive. Six months before they were due to sail, however, disaster struck. Sue woke up in the early hours of the morning to see Brian standing by the bed ashen as a ghost. He told her he had been in an accident.

'My first thought was, was Brian all right. Then I thought, *what about my car?*'

Brian had experienced a normal day at work. Having finished the late shift and clocked out, he climbed into the car and switched on the radio. It was late and he was thinking of bed. Further down the road he indicated right and then there was a terrific bang from behind. Someone had run into the car! A lot of thoughts went racing through his mind at once – the damage to the car, whether he was hurt, their planned holiday in France. . . . Later Brian's mother and Sue's father each offered their cars for the holiday, but Brian was not interested. He wanted to drive *his* car in France. Brian wanted the blue Sierra.

The vehicle was towed home. It was badly damaged, but they hoped it could be repaired. When the insurance assessor arrived, he did not hold out much hope and after a few weeks their insurance company duly confirmed that the car would be collected by a breaker's yard from Swindon in Wiltshire. The couple felt very sad, as Sue explained.

'We just felt guilty. The car had been so reliable, it never let us down once. I just took it for granted we were going to have it for a long time. It was our family car, a lovely old thing, and I was very sad to see it go.'

Before that happened, though, her brother-in-law, Ken, called round to remove some parts from the wreckage to use in his own car. While agreeing to this, a part of Sue saw it as desecration.

'I think it was because we'd taken such good care of it. The car was always polished and clean inside. Now it was all bashed in and we really didn't want it picked at. It was a strange feeling, but we felt like slapping Ken's hands to make him get off. It just seemed a shame, yet it was illogical, because the car was going to the scrap yard.'

Eventually the salvage company sent a flat-bed lorry, and Brian and Sue watched through the window as the wreckage was taken away. They bid a silent farewell to their shiny blue Sierra, and a while later Brian bought another car with the insurance money to take them to France.

It was a long journey from Somerset to Portsmouth, where they caught the ferry to St Malo, a twelve-hour crossing, and then four or five hours' ride through the French countryside to their camp site just north of Bordeaux. Brian said: 'It was nice to be in France, but it wasn't like driving my Sierra.'

They had been there five or six days when they saw the car.

'We were just popping out to get our daily supplies of bread, milk and things', Brian explained. 'I have a habit of reading number plates. As we were about to leave the camp site, I noticed two or three cars parked up. One of them was a blue Ford Sierra. I just happened to look down at the number plate – and there it was! I said to Sue, "There's our old Sierra." I said it so matter of fact and was going to drive on, but Sue made me stop.'

They climbed out of the car and went over to inspect the other vehicle. There was a young boy inside. Brian and Sue could not believe there eyes. They tapped on the window and asked the boy where his mum and dad were. The boy said they were in the shops.

When the owner came out and they told him the story, he took some convincing that the car really was the one they had parted with six months previously. Even he found it unbelievable that they should find their old car at the camp site where they had planned to take it before the smash. As Brian said: 'It was such a shock to see it on the same camp site in the same two weeks, in the same foreign country . . .'

Brian was able to point to things on the car that identified it as once belonging to him. Ken also came across and showed the new owner, Michael, where he had removed some items for his own car. Apparently Michael had bought the Sierra at an auction and had spent months repairing the damage. It had been bought with the intention of taking Michael and his family on holiday to France.

But that was not the end of the matter. The following week Sue and Brian went out for the day, and parked at a tourist spot. When they returned to the car park, there was the blue Ford Sierra standing right next to their car.

'We were astonished,' Sue said. 'It really felt as if the car was following us! I don't think the chap intentionally parked next to us. It was just another coincidence.'

EVEN STANDING STILL IT'S MOVING

IN April 1994 Citroën conducted an advertising campaign for the popular Xantia car with the slogan 'Even Standing Still It's Moving', referring to its aerodynamic design. Not long afterwards there were several reports of Xantias which had run away down hill after being parked. Drivers who experienced problems with the handbrake were advised to contact Transport Department safety investigators. Citroën denied that the handbrakes were faulty, but advised owners to put the vehicle in gear when parked on a slope.

TERMINAL BY NAME, TERMINAL BY NATURE

THE flash flood that hit Wenatchee, Washington, on 5 September 1925, was something the citizens were not likely to forget. It washed the foundations away from the three-storey wooden structure of the Springwater Hotel, which was then washed across a sixty-foot highway, where it collided with the Terminal Hotel.

ALARM CLOCK

IN his classic work *An Experiment with Time*, aviation pioneer J.W. Dunne relates an amazing personal experience. While he was staying at a Sussex hotel in 1899 he dreamed of an argument between himself and a waiter about the correct time. Dunne insisted it was 4.30 in the afternoon, while the waiter insisted it was 4.30 in the morning. The confusion was caused by Dunne's watch, which had stopped. In the dream he took it from his waistcoat pocket and saw the fingers were set at 4.30.

At this point he awoke and looked for his watch on the bed-side table, where it was usually placed at night, but found it was not there. Instead he discovered it on a chest of drawers and saw it had indeed stopped – at half past four.

Dunne rationalised the incident by assuming that the watch had stopped the previous afternoon and he had neglected to re-wind it. After noting the time, he then consciously forgot it. The dream was a way of reminding him. He re-wound the watch, but left the hands as they were because he was unsure of the time. Later that morning, when he went downstairs for breakfast, Dunne found a clock in order to set the watch at the correct time.

'To my absolute amazement', he wrote, 'I found that the hands had lost only some two or three minutes, *about the amount of time which had elapsed between waking from the dream and rewinding the watch.*'

Dunne now had a new theory. He suggested that the watch had actually stopped at the moment he had the dream. Even if it had stopped the previous afternoon, that he should dream of it precisely twelve hours later seemed too much for chance.

— ·12 · —

SMALL WORLD

Most people are familiar with the phrase 'It's a small world'. These words are usually uttered by friends or acquaintances who bump into one another in some far-off corner of the world. In the strange world of coincidences the phrase takes on an added dimension.

FOOD FOR THOUGHT

AUTHOR Camile Flammarion told a most remarkable story in his book *The Unknown*, published in 1902. It concerned his friend, the poet Emile Deschamps.

Plum pudding was an unknown in France during the nineteenth century. When he was at school in Orleans, Deschamps happened to share a table with a certain M. de Fortgibu, who had developed a taste for plum pudding after visiting England. He insisted that Deschamps try some.

Ten years later Deschamps was passing a restaurant when he happened to see a cook preparing a plum pudding. It reminded him of the first time he had tasted the dish and went inside to order some. Deschamps was told, however, that it was a special order, but perhaps the gentleman who had asked for it would allow him to have a slice? On turning round he discovered that 'the gentleman' was none other than his old school chum Fortgibu.

Many years later Deschamps was invited to a dinner at which plum pudding was served. This prompted the poet to tell his hosts about the remarkable coincidence involving Fortgibu. They all joked at the possibility of the old man turning up again. At which point there was a knock at the door and a servant announced the arrival of a guest. There in the doorway stood Fortgibu, astounded to see Deschamps – eating plum pudding.

After the shock had worn off, Fortgibu explained that he too had been invited out to dinner – but by someone else who had an apartment in the same building. The elderly man had mixed up the door numbers.

Deschamps commented: 'Three times in my life have I eaten plum pudding, and three times have I seen M. de Fortgibu!'

THE FOURTH EMERGENCY SERVICE

DURING the mid 1970s David Tebbutt's work often took him overseas. He was running a training course in Windsor when one of his students, who happened to work for the AA, approached him to ask a favour. The student had found out David was going to Nigeria the following week and asked him if he would pass on a note to his friend, John Colley, if he should run into him. Apparently Colley worked in Port Harcourt, but David was going to Lagos, so there was little likelihood of the two meeting. Nevertheless David took the note, placed it in his diary and promptly forgot about it.

When David arrived in Nigeria, he began to frequent a restaurant called Antoine's. On his third day there he went to the restaurant alone, but the place was almost full and so he had to share a table. Soon afterward a man arrived and sat down opposite David. While they were eating, David asked his dinner companion what had brought him to Lagos. The man replied that he worked in Port Harcourt and was only in the capital for the day; he added, by way of introduction, that his name was John Colley.

'Ah,' said David, 'I've got a message for you!'

A couple of years later David was a delegate on a course in Stevenage. During a meal in a nearby restaurant with some of his companions, David recounted the story, which caused some incredulity. After the meal they went to a local pub. There a man approached him and asked, 'Remember me?' It was the AA man.

David said he had passed on the note to John Colley. The former student said he already knew this as he had met John Colley in Stevenage – the previous week!

A TANGLED WEB

In 1973 Mrs W.M. Hamer and her friend went on holiday to Australia. Mrs Hamer intended visiting her daughter, while the other woman went to see her son and his family.

While they were in Australia, Mrs Hamer's friend's son invited them both to Canberra for the weekend. On the night of their arrival they were taken to see a colleague of the son's, only to find that he was just on his way out. He suggested that instead they visit his father-in-law, who was English, but had lived in Australia for some years.

The father-in-law, it transpired, had attended the same school as Mrs Hamer, who had known his sister. When she asked after his sister, he said that he had lost touch with her and asked if Mrs Hamer would make some enquiries for him on her return to England.

Back home Mrs Hamer and her friend went to book a hair appointment, but discovered that their usual hairdresser had closed down. Instead they booked into a new salon. During the appointment, the two ladies mentioned they had just come back from Australia. The hairdresser commented that she had an uncle there, but the family had lost touch with him. After further conversation the lost uncle turned out to be the man they had met! Mrs Hamer delightedly handed over his address.

CHANCE ENCOUNTER IN SWITZERLAND

IN 1972 Coral and Peter Alford from Chichester went on a caravan holiday touring Europe and stopped overnight in a small Swiss village. The couple decided they needed their hair doing and found a small hairdresser. Funnily enough the couple who owned the salon were English, but, even more intriguing, they were also named Alford! Furthermore the man's brother lived in Chichester and his telephone number was next to their's in the Portsmouth directory!

DESTINED TO MEET

IN August 1983 Mr and Mrs Jenkins from Leicestershire decided to visit their daughter who had moved to Edinburgh.

Mr Jenkins recollected that he had served in Egypt during World War II with a man called McKirdy, who had lived in Edinburgh. They had been out of touch for forty years and Mr Jenkins wondered if he could trace his wartime friend.

He had no idea whether McKirdy was alive or dead, or whether he had moved out of the area. At their daughter's house they looked in the telephone directory and were surprised to find only one entry for 'McKirdy'. Fearing embarrassment at ringing up the wrong man, the couple decided not to pursue the search and went off instead on a bus tour.

Upon arrival at the depot they were disappointed to learn that the tour had been cancelled owing to lack of bookings. Mrs Jenkins, therefore, went off to a telephone box near a taxi rank to call her daughter and explain what had happened. While she was doing so, her husband waited on the pavement. Moments later a taxi pulled up right beside him. As is the custom in Edinburgh, the driver's name was on the door. The name was McKirdy. As Mr Jenkins was astonished to discover, it was indeed his old chum from the RAF.

AT THE MEAT COUNTER

DOREEN Frost had never known her brother and sisters because in 1943 she was adopted at the age of two when her mother died. In January 1995 she was shopping in Southsea and was about to catch a bus home when, on impulse, she decided to buy some meat. She went into Dewhurst's and waited patiently to be served. But there was someone else in the queue who had also decided to enter the butcher's at the last moment. Barbara Small was on the way to pay her electricity bill and had decided to call in for some meat *en route*.

As Barbara glanced over her shoulder at the other people in the shop she saw Doreen and noticed a family resemblance. 'We were both in green,' she said, 'and looked very much alike.' Barbara had been twelve when Doreen had left the family for adoption.

Something convinced her it was her baby sister Doreen, who she had last seen fifty-two years earlier. She said to the stranger, 'Is your name Doreen?' She looked at Barbara and replied, 'Yes, but I don't know you.' Barbara countered, 'You should do. I am your sister!'

There followed a tearful reunion outside the shop where the women talked for three hours. When Doreen was adopted, she was brought up in Cosham with two adopted brothers and a sister. As a child she was unaware of her adoption and ignorant of the fact that her real family were living just two miles away. The families never kept in touch and both thought the other had moved away from the area.

The sisters believe they were fated to meet that day.

ON THE WAY TO THE WEDDING

ANN Seeliger, who was from a small village in South Africa, decided to come to England for a holiday. Whilst in London she went to do some shopping on Oxford Street. As she was walking along, gazing into the shop windows, she was approached by a pleasant-looking young couple, who explained that they were on their way to get married at a registry office and needed a witness. Would Ann volunteer? She agreed. Then the couple stopped a young man in his twenties and asked him if he would act as their second witness. He too agreed and so the small party boarded a bus for the five-minute ride to the registrar's.

On the bus Ann sat next to the second witness and in the course of casual conversation discovered to their immense surprise that, although the young man's family had lived in the UK for many years, he had in fact been born in the same village in South Africa where Ann Seeliger still lived! Indeed, she had known his parents very well before they emigrated and could clearly recall his mischievousness as a tiny child.

THE GIRL IN THE BOAT

THIS is a beautiful haunting story. It began in 1958 when twenty-year-old Jim Adams decided to visit London for a holiday. He had rarely travelled outside of the North-East before, but in a few months he would be faced with the choice of doing National Service or joining the merchant navy. It seemed an opportune time to spread his wings and see the Big City.

He bought a few extra things to take, but his prize possession was a new Kodak Brownie box camera. Jim carried it around with him everywhere in London and took the usual shots of Trafalgar Square, Buckingham Palace and Big Ben. One hot day Jim was weary of trudging around the London streets and decided to take a boat trip on the River Thames, where he hoped it would be cooler and he could relax.

The young man boarded a boat at Westminster which was heading up the Thames. As the boat chugged away from the city centre the scenery began to change. While travelling through Thames Ditton Jim took some photographs. Suddenly he was captured by the vision of a young girl in a small boat. She looked about twelve.

'As we passed her I picked up the camera. She had seen me standing on the deck and must have realised I was about to take a photograph, because she looked towards me. I don't actually know what possessed me to do it. Here was a little girl on her own rowing a boat in a wide, fast-flowing river. It seemed so unusual.'

A few days later Jim returned home with four exposed black-and-white films. It was almost two years before he had them processed, because at the time he did not have the money. By then his brother, Ken, was training as a photographer and he managed to get them done for him. Among the many shots of tourist attractions was the photograph of the girl in the boat. They were all carefully stored in a cardboard box and then put away.

Ken Adams worked at a studio in Sunderland and was a very keen photographer. After he had finished his apprenticeship he got a job as a ship's photographer and spent the next two years sailing around the world. On his return to England he found a job in Surbiton, Surrey. One day, while he was busy working in the dark room, doing some commercial printing, his boss appeared in the gloom with a young lady.

'He introduced her to me and said she was joining the firm. That was how I met Heather. It was love at first sight. We felt very passionate about one another from that first day.'

They courted for two years and then married. In 1987, on a Bank Holiday weekend, Ken went back up to Sunderland to visit his brother. In conversation the subject of holidays came up and this started them reminiscing about Jim's trip to London almost thirty years earlier. Out came the photographs and they began going through them. As Ken browsed, they reminded him of the time he spent printing them while the boss was out of the studio.

'Jim was pointing out different places in London and I recognised one of them as being on the river near Thames Ditton. Then I saw the girl in the boat *and I knew it was my wife.*'

Ken had developed the picture of the girl in the boat eight

years before they met. Thames Ditton was where his wife's family lived. He had listened to them reminiscing about the times she spent on the river as a little girl. He had also transferred the family's old cine films on to Super 8.

Ken could not wait until he got home to tell Heather of the amazing coincidence, so he phoned her from Jim's house. She afterwards confirmed that it was her in the picture.

'I knew it was me because I always used to get into the dinghy first when we came home from school. I would row around one side of Thames Ditton Island and come back with the current on the far side. When I saw the photograph, I was totally amazed!'

Heather actually recollected the picture being taken.

'I remember someone standing up on the deck with his camera. This wasn't unusual because most tourists liked to photograph one of the gardens which was probably the most beautiful on the river. But this man was facing in the opposite direction and took a snap of me.'

Ken summed it up in this way: 'When you think of the distance we lived apart and our different family backgrounds, the chances of me arriving in that small town and getting a job, and Heather working for the same firm – coupled with Jim taking that photograph – it really makes you wonder if there was a guiding hand in it all.'

NOT MISSED ON THE MISSISSIPPI

GWYN and Margaret Jones were married in February 1951. Among their wedding guests was a friend and colleague of Margaret's by the name of Lorna Abel. Shortly after the wedding, however, Lorna moved to Dorset and they lost touch with her.

'I met Lorna while we were both working in the sales office of a spring manufacturing plant in West Bromich', Margaret explained. 'We were great friends and I naturally invited her to our wedding. When Lorna moved away, we completely lost touch with her. All we knew was that she and her husband ran a pub somewhere in Dorset.'

Gwyn and Margaret loved to travel, and in early 1996 they booked a holiday touring around the southern states of America. They were booked into a hotel in New Orleans for a couple of days and arranged to go on a steamer down the Mississippi.

As they boarded the steamer, the tour guide said there was another party from England so they might bump into someone they knew. The guide was only joking, of course, but, as it happened, she was speaking the truth. As the boat returned to the quayside, they were queueing on the gang plank to disembark when they became aware of a woman standing in front of them.

'The lady in front of us must have heard our English accents,' Margaret explained, 'because she turned around. It was amazing! I recognised her immediately – even though we hadn't set eyes on each other for nearly half a century.

'Lorna knew who I was straight away. I was so stunned I didn't know what to say. I just screamed, "It's Lorna Abel!" Gwyn was speechless too.'

Margaret reflected that, if they had been further back in the queue, they might never have met up with Lorna.

SCHOFIELD AND SCHOFIELD

WHEN newly-weds Harry and Barbara Schofield set up home in a small flat on Albert Lane, Morley, Yorkshire, and found that the couple living above them were also called Schofield, they thought it was just coincidence.

That was in 1953, and after six months they moved into a house in Mill Street on the other side of town. When they decided to have a family, the couple moved to a larger property in nearby Gilderstone. There they raised seven children before retiring to a cosy council bungalow, 83 Ingle Avenue, Morley.

In the meantime the other Schofields – Rowland and Madge – left their flat in Albert Road shortly after Harry and Barbara, and moved to Asquith Avenue in Morley. A few years later they bought a house in Ardsley a few miles away, where they stayed until moving into number 81 Ingle Avenue.

Neither couple had any idea that their lives had come full circle until Harry spotted a familiar figure carrying some boxes into the house next door.

'I looked up from my flowerbeds and saw Rowland,' Harry explained. 'I recognised him straight away and wondered what he was doing here. When he told me he and Madge were moving in, I thought he must be joking!'

Rowland commented: 'After we moved from Albert Lane all those years ago we did see them now and again. Harry and I used to play in the same pub darts team, but over the years we totally lost touch. It's great to be back living so close to them. We always got on very well.'

It was the other Schofield – Harry – who put it all into perspective: 'There are literally thousands of council flats and bungalows in Leeds and Morley. The chances of us ending up living next door to one another after all this time must be one in a million.'

When you add to that calculation the coincidence of the Schofield name, the chances must be astronomical.

− ·13 · −

RINGING SUCCESSES

It should come as no surprise that a common and intrusive communications system – such as the telephone – should feature in some quite odd coincidences.

ADVANCE NUMBER

A Mrs Stoker became embroiled in a mystery which began two years previously. At that time her daughter Beverly kept complaining that a series of numbers kept running through her head. Beverly wrote the numbers down and then forgot about them.

When Mrs Stoker moved to Leek in Staffordshire, she was given a new telephone number as she was now connected to a different exchange. She rang Beverly to give her the number, and her daughter said it sounded familiar. Beverly checked her mother's new telephone number with the digits she had written down two years previously – they were identical.

INDIRECT LINE

KATIE McKellar works from an agency. At the beginning of March 1996 she received a telephone call from a girl she did not know. Apparently the girl was in a fix and she had been recommended to call Katie by a mutual friend. She had been hired to do some work in a marquee in Battersea, London, but at the last minute discovered her car would not work. Could Katie help her out and do the job for her?

Katie agreed and then decided to telephone her husband at work to inform him where she was going. When she explained the situation, he was astounded. Apparently a young woman had called his workplace earlier and he had taken the call. She had apologised and said she was unable to make it to Battersea because her car had broken down, but she was trying to find a replacement. He told her she must have dialled the wrong number and thought no more of it.

DIRECT LINE

IN July 1970 Mr George Whiting's youngest son, Neil, was on a school camping trip in the South of France. Mr Whiting had arranged to meet Neil at the end of his trip outside the RAC Centre in Paris, so he could then join the rest of the family for an additional week's holiday before returning to school.

Unfortunately Mr Whiting's other son, Edward, aged twenty, suddenly developed acute appendicitis, which meant the family would be unable to rendezvous with Neil as planned. The other problem was that they did not have a contact telephone number nor a full address for the camp. All they knew was that the site was near a village called Vallon.

Mr Whiting contacted the International Telephone Exchange and they told him they would make some enquiries. An hour later they called Mr Whiting and suggested he call a small café in Vallon, the number of which he was given, and ask the owner if he or she knew the camp site number or could help get a message through.

He rang the café immediately and a voice answered, so Mr Whiting asked if the person spoke English and said he was trying to trace someone urgently. The person at the other end said he was English and asked who was he trying to trace? Mr Whiting gave the details. A long silence followed. After a while Mr Whiting asked if he was still there. The reply came: 'Is that you, Dad? It's Neil here.'

Apparently Neil and a number of his friends had become friendly with the woman who owned the café and often spent a lot of time there. When the telephone had rung, the owner was busy and had asked Neil to answer it!

REVERSED CHARGE

RIKKI Brown went out with his brother to celebrate his birthday in East Kilbride, Scotland. At about two in the morning they decided to walk home and reached a junction where Rikki went one way and his brother the other. Rikki had only gone about twenty yards when he heard a thud, followed by a cry of pain. His brother had slipped on ice and could not move. Rikki found a callbox and telephoned his brother's wife, explained the predicament and asked her to pick them up. As he did not have any change for the call, Rikki reversed the charges.

Two months later he was in his car when his pager sounded.

He parked at the side of the nearest telephone box to call his place of work. It was the box he had used on the night of his brother's accident. As he approached it the telephone started ringing. He picked it up and, to his amazement, found his brother on the other end.

Apparently he had received his telephone bill and could not remember accepting a reversed charge call, so he had called the number out of curiosity. Rikki commented that East Kilbride has a population of about 250,000 people and a bustling town centre with numerous telephone boxes.

GETTING YOUR FAX RIGHT

JASON Pegler worked for the AA in Dover as a salesman. When he finished work on this particular night, he left a colleague called Sue in charge. Later he was walking through Folkestone when he heard the telephone ringing in one of the boxes on the street. On impulse he picked it up and heard Sue's voice on the other end!

'Hello, Jason,' she said, 'it's Sue. The fax machine isn't working.'

Jason was flabbergasted and tried to explain to her that he was speaking from a callbox. At first she did not understand; then it sank in. How had it happened?

Apparently Sue had looked up Jason's employee records to find his telephone number when she experienced trouble with the fax machine. But, instead of his phone number, she dialled his staff number and prefixed it with the area code. The first five digits were identical to the number of the call box. This was incredible enough but, given Jason was walking past the box at that exact moment and should decide to answer the phone, make the odds astronomical.

HAPPY BIRTHDAY TO YOU
– AND YOU . . .

WHEN the telephone rang at Jan Morris's home in Llanystumdwy, Gwynedd on 2 October 1992, the message she received was not a surprise, although the callers were. Without introduction a man and a woman began singing 'Happy Birthday To You . . .' That was fine as it was indeed Jan's birthday, except that they addressed the greeting to someone called 'Denis'. It turned out the couple had dialled the wrong number!

IT'S FOR YOO HOO!

STUDENT nurse Kathleen Chapman started work at 7 am on the children's ward and went about her routine as normal. At around lunchtime she was asked to take some prescriptions to the pharmacy in the main hospital building. An hour or so later she returned to the pharmacy to pick up the drugs.

The route took her along a corridor that branched off to the right. At this point Kathleen could hear a telephone ringing. The sound was coming from a public phone in the corridor. Although it is not something she would normally do, she picked up the receiver and said 'Hello'. It was a man's voice at the other end and one she recognised – her grandad's.

'Hello, Kath,' Grandad said, 'is your mum there?'

Kathleen was bemused and could not understand why he had telephoned the hospital when he could call her mother at home. He said that, when he had spoken to her mother earlier, she had told him to call her in half an hour. In her confusion, Kathleen wondered why her mother was coming to the hospital. The conversation became even more confused when Kathleen told her grandad she was speaking to him from work. He became annoyed and put the telephone down on her.

When she arrived back at the ward, Kathleen called her mother at home and explained what had happened. Apparently Mrs Bowring had been looking after her father that morning because he had a heart condition. When she left the old man's house, she told him to phone her in half an hour if he was feeling unwell. He had called the hospital by mistake, even though he did not have the number.

Later Kathleen checked her home number against the number on the corridor telephone and discovered it was one digit different. Kathleen believes her grandad must have misdialled her home number. But that does not adequately explain the mystery, as Kathleen pointed out. 'For me to be in that corridor at that time and then to actually pick up the receiver must be one in a million.'

– · 14 · –

PREDICTABLE

People who apparently predict the future attract a lot of attention – and controversy. When they get things right, is it 'coincidence' or a genuine psychic ability? Sceptics will argue that the law of probability dictates that, out of all the dreams remembered on a particular night, one or more will match a real event which afterwards occurs.

There are two types of predictions. Those that happen by accident, and those that are made by design.

ACCIDENTAL PREDICTIONS

WE have all heard someone say he or she would like to dream the winning combination of the football pools or the national lottery. In July 1975 shop assistant Mary Redding of Stirchley, Birmingham had such a dream. Five days later she was given a cheque by Vernon's Pools for £132,631!

Dr John Beloff, a parapsychologist from Edinburgh

University, made a study of Mrs Gwen Bridgland of Barrow-in-Furness, who had several prophetic dreams. In one dream she found herself on a train which stopped. She then watched some men unloading large amounts of money. A few days later came the Great Train Robbery.

A train featured again in a dream she had on 2 September 1970. She was standing on a crowded railway station and watched a man jump to his death in front of a moving train. In the dream she commented to her husband: 'Its probably for the best anyway, Geoff. The man was wanted for a sex murder.' She sent details of the dream to Beloff on 5 September. Eleven days later a girl was sexually assaulted and murdered in Broxbourne, Hertfordshire. On 19 September the man believed to be responsible for the crime died under a train.

Shawn Robbins, a twenty-eight-year-old American, had a vivid dream in February 1974. He saw a large aircraft bound for London crashing, killing hundreds and leaving no survivors. Among the victims was a member of the United States diplomatic service and his wife. He also 'knew' that it would happen in either March or May. On 3 March a DC 10, flying from Paris to London, crashed in France killing all 346 on board. This included US Cultural Attaché Wayne Wilcox and his wife.

A dream of death that came true, except for one crucial detail, was reported by Mrs Frances Whaley from Cockenzie, East Lothian.

In the dream her daughter Byrnice had toothache. Mrs Whaley tried telephoning several dentists and found one in Musselburgh who agreed to treat her. The place was an old house with an ornate ceiling in the waiting room. When she took Byrnice to the toilet down a gloomy passage, she noticed chess board style lino on the floor and saw a bath standing on ornate feet. As the dream unfolded Mrs Whaley returned to the waiting room, while Byrnice went into the surgery. A friend appeared and the pair chatted until the surgery door opened and the dentist appeared. In the dream he said: 'I'm sorry, but your daughter has died under anaesthetic.' Mrs Whaley woke up crying, but after a week or so forgot about the dream. Some months later Byrnice woke up with a terrible toothache. Her mother telephoned several dentists, but the only one who could fit her in at short notice was in Musselburgh. Even when she saw the ornate ceiling and the chequered black-and-white floor Mrs Whaley still did not remember the dream.

While Byrnice was in the surgery, a friend of her mother's came into the waiting room and the two women began to chat. Then it happened. The dentist opened the door and walked into the waiting room. At that second Mrs Whaley remembered the dream in its full horror. The dentist began to speak.

'I'm sorry, but I can't take out Byrnice's tooth. She's got a cold.'

Mrs Whaley grabbed Byrnice and fled. The girl's tooth was taken out two days later – by another dentist.

Author Theo Aronson had a strong 'feeling' that something was going to happen to his manuscript. But, ironically, if he had taken the line of action he was contemplating, disaster assuredly would have struck.

He was living at the time in Durban, South Africa, and was working on what was to be his first published book, *The Golden Bees*. He had written out the first draft in long hand on a scribbler pad. Having finished writing, he went away on holiday to see his parents. As soon as he reached their home, however, he became increasingly concerned at having left the sole draft of the book unprotected in his apartment. If anything were to happen to it while he was away, it would be irreplaceable.

His mother, seeing how worried Theo was, suggested that he

ring the couple in the appartment below his, who had a spare key, and ask them to retrieve the manuscript, keeping it in a safe place until his return. Although this seemed a good idea, he came to the conclusion that he was probably worrying about nothing and so decided not to contact his neighbours.

As Theo found on his return to Durban, he had made the right decision: 'I discovered to my horror that, while my apartment was safe and sound, and my book secure, my neighbours' place had been thoroughly vandalised and burgled.'

In early February 1981 Lee Fields and her soldier husband moved to Germany. The move went with the job, but after less than two weeks Lee was already missing her friends and relations in England. It was then that she had the dream.

Despite the fact Lee could not drive, she was at the steering wheel of her husband's new car, cruising down a familiar road in Liverpool. Then she spotted James, one of her brothers, standing at the edge of the pavement. He was dressed in a sombre black suit, gazing at her as if she were part of a funeral cortège. Next to him stood her father. He wore a plain grey suit and stood to attention with a deadpan expression on his face.

Lee swung the car over to them and climbed out. She approached her brother and asked him what was wrong with 'Dad'. James looked at her with a vaguely wistful look in his eyes, but he said nothing. Then she turned to her father and asked him what was the matter. To her horror and amazement he suddenly crumpled to his knees and wrapped his arms around his only daughter. Tears streamed down his face as he begged her to stay.

Of course she realised it was 'only a dream', but she wondered if something was amiss back home. A telephone call would do no harm. Lee was very close to her father, but she reasoned that the dream was just a reflection of her homesickness. She put off the call, telling herself that, if anything was wrong, she would have heard by now. When she did eventually hear, the news shocked her.

Her father had been taken seriously ill on the morning of her dream. He was currently in hospital, although no one knew what the outcome would be. She at once took a flight back to England, and her brother's stony expression when he met her was precisely as it had been in the dream. Her father was already dead – she was just too late to see him. If she had only telephoned upon waking. . . .

PREDICTIONS BY DESIGN

FROM the moment she learned to talk Cassy Holmes from Sheffield could apparently predict the future. Before she was five the little girl accurately predicted that a picture would fall off a wall two minutes before it actually did so, that her grandfather's best friend was about to die, and that an aircraft carrying Vietnamese orphans would crash. When Cassy told her mother that relatives were about to arrive, her mother always put the kettle on because she knew Cassy was telling the truth. When asked for an explanation, Cassy replied that she 'just knew it'.

An eighteen-year-old American student by the name of Lee Fried came up with some remarkably accurate predictions. He wrote them on a card on 20 March 1977, which was placed in an envelope sealed with wax. This was kept locked away in the office of Terry Sandford, President of Duke University, North Carolina, where Fried was a student. Eight days later the envelope was opened live on television.

Fried said that two Boeing 747s would crash and 583 people would lose their lives. On 27 March two Boeings did indeed collide at Tenerife and 582 people died. Fried was out by one death.

He predicted that the university basketball team would lose the last match of the season to Marquette by sixty-eight to fifty-eight. He was right – they did lose, but the score was sixty-seven to fifty-nine. Fried had also written that the television presenter would wear a lavender suit with cream blouse and silver earings, and that the Supreme Court would hear four cases on capital punishment – which were both correct.

Self-proclaimed 'psychic astrologer' Jack Gillen made a plane crash prediction on two different radio stations in Florida. He said that on 12 December 1977 there would be an air crash at Evansville, Indiana. In fact a DC 3 did crash at Evansville – on 13 December, killing all twenty-nine people on board.

This next prediction had a sting in the tale – or was it just coincidence?

John Snell of Poole in Dorset was told by a palm reader that he would die on his forty-fifth birthday. For years the long-distance lorry driver ignored the warning, smoking and drinking his way towards destiny. However, during the year leading up to his forty-fifth birthday, he began to worry and cut out his vices. On his birthday he stayed at home, watching the hours tick by.

Two days later the death of John Snell of Poole was reported in the local newspaper on his forty-fifth birthday. The palmist was right after all – and wrong too. There were two John Snells in Poole – who had lived only 100 yards apart. The John Snell whose palm had been read was still alive.

– · 15 · –
ODDITIES

Here are some stories which do not seem to fit into any of the previous categories. We start with a story about pigeons. If the observations of some human travellers on the London Underground are correct, then be prepared to give up your seat occasionally to one of our feathered friends. . . .

PIGEON FANCIERS

PIGEONS, it seems, are not dim-witted birds, but possess a prowess and intelligence equal to man – and that's official! After VE Day in 1945 the People's Dispensary for Sick Animals awarded fifty-three bronze Dicken Medals – the animal equivalent of VCs – for gallantry while serving with the armed forces. Thirty-one of these medals went to pigeons.

Bravest was 'Mary' from Exeter, who flew from 1940 until the end of the war. During one flight she vanished for a week, but finally arrived with her message, severely injured after being

attacked by a hawk. 'Ruhr Express' was parachuted into the
Ruhr pocket more than 300 miles from base. His delivery of a
valuable message in record time during April 1945 was con-
sidered to have had a direct bearing on the progress of the war.
'William of Orange' covered 260 miles – 135 of which were over
rough seas – in four hours and twenty-five minutes, an average
speed of almost sixty miles per hour.

As if this were not proof enough, there is evidence that
pigeons are using the Underground to travel across London and
save their wings! It began when Rachel Robinson of Bayswater
wrote to *New Scientist* magazine and described how she had seen
a pigeon board a tube train and get off at the next stop. Other
witnesses described how the birds were deliberately hopping on
board. Lorna Read described how one passenger tried to deter a
pigeon by shooing it out. As the doors were closing, it made one
final frantic effort to enter – just like humans who sometimes
throw themselves at the doors as they shut.

Jack Howlett from Oxford said that he had often travelled in
the company of a pigeon on the tube from Paddington. Sabiha
Foster of Benfleet, Essex made the following observation: 'A pair
of pigeons hopped on to the Circle Line at Aldgate, stayed by
the door and alighted with purpose at the next stop – Tower Hill.
How did they know the platform for Tower Hill was the same
side as that for Aldgate?'

TROUBLE WITH WIND

A SINGLE blast of wind totally destroyed a huge train engine
shed at 3.30 pm on Friday 30 October 1863. The building
belonged to the London, Brighton and South Coast Railway at

New Cross in South London. It was 145 feet long and 42 feet wide. Although strongly built of fourteen-inch thick brickwork and strengthened by twenty-three-inch buttresses every twenty-one feet, the wind reduced it to rubble in seconds.

The doors were open at the time and the sudden gust, unable to escape from the confined space, lifted up the roof and blasted the walls asunder. Then the roof fell upon the debris.

There were seven locomotives in the shed at the time. Number 111 was derailed and overturned. The driver and fireman escaped injury by diving into the pit beneath the engine, but a cleaner was crushed to death.

CAUGHT ON CAMERA

JOHN Colley was in his local pub in Sutton Coldfield when he struck up a conversation with a stranger. The other man had recently moved into the area and had found in his loft some cans of old 16mm film which he was going to get rid of. John used to collect vintage film and still had his motorised viewer, so he offered to look through the cans.

The task took quite a while and John learned a lot about the previous occupants of the bungalow. While watching one section of film, he came across a sequence set in a fairground. It was the Onion Fair at the Serpentine Ground in Aston, Birmingham. John recalled going to these fairs in his childhood. Imagine his surprise when he saw two boys walk into the frame and realised they were himself and a schoolfriend!

The film was taken in 1953 and his parents had never taken photographs, so he treasures this early picture of himself. John remembers seeing a man at the fair with a camera and wondering at the time if he was going to be on the local news. He feels that seeing the camera sparked off his interest in photography, which later extended to moving film.

Jim Willis found pictures of himself on top of a pile of rubbish. One Sunday morning in the mid 1980s he was walking through Shannon Park in Belfast when he saw some brown envelopes. He picked them up because they were still dry, and he thought that maybe they had been dropped, possibly stolen and discarded in a hurry. Written on the envelopes were shutter speeds and exposure times, and inside were hundreds of negatives.

Coincidentally, Jim possessed an interest in photography and had a dark room at home. He took the negatives back, but did not develop them for a couple of years.

When he did start work on them, he began to get a strange feeling. The 200 or so negatives produced images of Esso garages in the region, a man on a motorbike and a few beach shots of a man reading a newspaper dated 1951. They all seemed to have been taken at around that time.

One picture showed a family scene outside a house. In the window was an ornament depicting a small boy holding a fishing rod. Jim recognised it as one his grandmother used to have in the window of her house. On further examination he recognised a small girl in another picture. It was his cousin Kathleen, when she was five or six, now living in Canada. In fact several of the pictures depicted family members. He had often wished he had more photographs of relations on his father's side and now he did!

When Kathleen came over for a visit she confirmed it was her in the picture, but could not remember any of them being taken. No one in the family can recall them being taken. The shots look as if they have been taken by a professional or someone very interested in photography, but no one can think who. . . .

FAIR EXCHANGE

KATIE McKellar from Chiswick in London was working with a team of girls at Heathrow Airport. They were on a rota which covered different terminals. Upon finishing her shift one day she checked her schedule to see where and when she was next working. To her horror Katie discovered she had done the wrong shift. But she could not understand why the girl who should have been there had not turned up or why no one had telephoned to find out why her duty was not covered. When Katie made some enquiries, she discovered that, by a bizarre twist, Jackie, the other girl, had done a direct swop with her. Both girls had gone to the wrong terminal without realising it.

TAKE OFF

CATHERINE Walker reported on an apt coincidence that befell her father in May 1990. He had decided to visit the grave of his brother who had died during World War II and was buried at Binbrook, Lincolnshire. It was the first time he had returned to Binbrook since the funeral.

Upon arrival at the cemetery he happened to notice smoke rising in the distance. As he attended to his brother's grave fire engines drove past, sounding their alarms. That evening he discovered the cause. Apparently the RAF station at Binbrook had been closed down, but the aerodrome was being used by director David Puttnam to make a film about the American forces in World War II called *Memphis Belle*. During filming a plane which had been taking off had crashed at the end of the runway, bursting into flames. The crew escaped without injury.

This mirrored the aircraft accident that killed his brother forty-seven years before. He had been taking off at Binbrook when the aircraft crashed on the runway. In his case, however, the aircraft was loaded with ammunition ready for a mission to Germany. The ensuing fire had caused a massive explosion that had killed all the crew.

When Catherine's father returned home to Bath, he saw an article in the local paper about the film being made in Binbrook. David Puttnam lived in nearby Chippenham.

A QUESTION OF FAITH

IN late 1972 or early 1973 Jonathan Tetherly and his wife of Chicopee, Massachusetts were talking with friends in their studio apartment. The apartment was on the campus of a Christian seminary. For no reason he is aware of Jonathan suddenly said: 'I wonder what the beliefs of the Hari Krishnas are?'

Although they had all seen Hari Krishnas in Boston a few miles away, they were hardly a normal topic of conversation. However no sooner had Jonathan asked the question than there was a knock at the door. There stood a Hari Krishna selling books about his faith. Nervously they all laughed, but, because he had just raised the question about their beliefs, Jonathan felt he had no choice but to buy a book.

Later he pondered the coincidence and thought it highly unlikely that Hari Krishnas would venture into a Christian seminary.

SEEN BUT NOT HEARD

A ROUND 1992 Channel 4's *Travelogue* series recorded a feature on Chile. It was for inclusion in the last progamme of that season. As part of that feature Robert Elms interviewed a Chilean woman who claimed she was a witch.

When the production crew returned to England, they discovered that the filmed interview with the witch had lost its sound. This was despite the fact that the sound recordist had checked the sound on tape at the time of the interview. Everything else on the tape was fine. As the woman was speaking in Spanish, it was decided to use the interview anyway, but with a voice-over.

When the programme came to be broadcast, the Crystal Palace transmitter broke down as the section featuring the witch began. As it ended, the transmitter came back on again. The transmission tape had been checked beforehand and it was all right.

The production team were blissfully unaware of the glitch as they were holding an end-of-series party at the time. Because the party was in a café which did not have TV reception, the producer decided to bring in a monitor and video-player to show the programme simultaneously with transmission. As the moment arrived for the interview with the witch, the sound disappeared and only returned when that section had finished.

Apparently, when the series was repeated, once again the final programme suffered transmission difficulties during the witch's interview.

THE APRIL FOOL

A YOUNG woman born on April Fool's Day 1971 has been leading the authorities in America quite a dance. Birdie Jo is the dark half of twins with the appropriate surname of Hoaks. Her latest caper in December 1995 was to pose as a thirteen-year-old boy called Michael Ross in Vermont. Hoaks claimed that 'he' had been abandoned at a bus stop in Salt Lake City, Utah, by 'his' stepmother just before Christmas. 'He' produced a birth certificate and a letter purportedly written by the step-mother. It described how she was unable to care for the boy because the child's father had AIDS and his real mother was dead.

The story received massive news coverage. However, when the authorities contacted their counterparts in Utah, the game was up. Hoaks had pulled the stunt before, but a routine medical check had revealed her to be a twenty-three-year-old woman, and she had served the same number of days in prison. In fact she had a police record twenty pages long, detailing cons carried out in ten other states.

In Vermont police sergeant Ron Elwell said: 'She may be a transient, but she knows the system. She knows how to get free lodging and food.'

THE QUEENS' MYSTERY MESSAGE

IN 1978 a double mystery involving the SS *Queen Mary* and the SS *Queen Elizabeth II* (or *QE2* as she is affectionately known) was made public. Radio Officer Alan Holmes was on duty aboard the *QE2*, which was sailing across the Atlantic to

America, when he received the following coded message: 'GKS GBTT QSX AREA 1A'.

Alan realised at once that the code was one which was no longer in use. When he deciphered the message, Alan discovered it was a routine position check from the old liner *Queen Mary* to the Portishead Radio at Burnham in Somerset. This threw up a number of anomalies.

The *Queen Mary* had been sold over eleven years earlier to the City of Long Beach, California as a floating conference centre. Before the old coding system had been abandoned the *QE2* had inherited the 'GKS' call sign. So, if the message were one transmitted from the *Queen Mary* at least eleven years previously, where had it been all that time? And what a coincidence that her successor should be in the right place to pick it up. . . .

When Alan Holmes was interviewed by the media, he speculated that the original signal had bounced off an object in space light years away and that they had been lucky to be in the right position to pick it up on its return. The Portishead Radio station manager, Donald Mulholland, was more sceptical, however. He thought it was too much of a coincidence that the *QE2*, of all ships, should be in the right place to pick up the signal; he thought the most likely explanation was that someone had sent a hoax message.

By this time Mr Holmes was fed up with the whole affair and said the only reason he had reported it was because he was not alone in the radio room when the signal came in. He thought the hoax hypothesis highly unlikely. Someone would have had to go to a lot of trouble, plus they would have needed to know the exact frequency he was listening on and when.

SITE SEEING

During one of his holidays to England from South Africa author Theo Aronson hired a car and went off to do some sightseeing. In a country town he had never before visited he was obliged to stop to buy something from a shop. On his return to the car park he found the vehicle would not start. As the battery seemed to be dead, he called out the AA to replace it.

Many years later he bought a charming house in a small country town. Only after he had moved in did Theo discover that the precise spot on the car park where he had broken down overlooked his new home.

THE COINCIDENCE THAT WASN'T
– OR WAS IT?

Mr Ron Parker from Middlesbrough, Cleveland had a weird experience on 21 June 1965, as he told the magazine *Fortean Times*. At that time he had just bought his first car and had decided one day to take his wife and two daughters out for a picnic. Not far out of Middlesbrough they stopped at a ruined castle and church, where lies the tomb of a crusader. His daughters wanted to see inside the tomb, so he lifted them up to peer through the grille in the door. Suddenly Mrs Parker screamed out as a man touched her on the shoulder. None of them had seen the man approach, even though the path was covered in gravel.

The man appeared very distressed and was crying. When Ron asked him what was wrong, the man requested that they follow him through the church yard. He stopped and asked them to approach a certain tombstone, read the inscription, then return and repeat it to him. The inscription read: 'Here lies the body of Harold James Bell of Silloth, Cumberland. Born 21 June 1815. Died 21 June 1865, aged fifty years.'

When they repeated this to him, the stranger broke down completely. Not until he had regained some of his composure was he able to explain what was wrong. His name, he said, was also Harold James Bell of Silloth, Cumberland, born on 21 June 1915, and today was his fiftieth birthday. He was a sales representative for a Cumberland company and that very morning had been requested to work the Middlesbrough area – a place he was totally unfamiliar with. Five miles away some force had compelled him to turn off the main road and drive down the network of country lanes until he reached the church. He had been pushed and shoved up the path until he reached the tombstone.

Mr Bell was convinced that this was a way of telling him he had come to the end of his life, and nothing Mr and Mrs Parker could say convinced him otherwise. Ron escorted him to his car, a 1964 Ford Anglia Estate, and noted carpet samples and bits of paperwork inside.

The following Monday Ron told his boss at work the tale. A week later his boss came in to the office laughing and complimented Ron on making up such a good story. He and his wife had visited the church, and could not find the tombstone. Ron was amazed, as it really could not be overlooked. After work he drove up to the church himself and, sure enough, there was no sign of the stone. Ron Parker wrote: 'I always wonder what became of the unhappy Mr Bell. Did he and his car really exist that day? Our conversation, the atmosphere and the unreality of it all made this the strangest happening in my life.'

— ·16· —
CURSED OR COINCIDENCE?

In the world of coincidence it is interesting to note how certain objects or people attract more than their fair share of tragedy. In such cases we tend to say that they are 'cursed', that some sort of spell or mark of bad luck has been placed upon them. Take the example of the Mississippi packet *Jo Davies*.

It sank after only three trips and its engines were then installed in the steamboat *Reindeer*. That sank after four trips, and the engines were then transferred to the *Reindeer II* – which also disappeared beneath the Mississippi after four trips. They were then fitted to the *Colonel Clay* – which sank after two trips. The message not having yet got through, the engines were given to the ss *Monroe*, which was destroyed by fire. Finally the engines were installed in a mill in Elizabeth Town, which was rased to the ground. . . .

TWELVE HOLES IN ONE!

BOB Waldron, an area manager for Goodyear, only started playing golf in 1994. He joined the Three Hammers Golf Club in Coven Heath, Staffordshire, when he was fifty. Most golfers spend a lifetime waiting in vain for that magical moment when their tee shot disappears into a hole. But by June 1996 Bob had scored twelve holes-in-one – in just thirteen months. His achievement rocked the golfing community.

The club's resident professional, Shaun Ball, has only scored six holes-in-one, in six years. He said: 'When the PGA championships were played here last year, eighty pros each played thirty-six holes. Not one of them hit a hole-in-one. That puts Bob's feat in context. The odds must be millions to one – and every ace has been verified.'

Bob was modest about his success. 'I can't explain how I have managed it – I guess I must be lucky.'

REBEL WITH A CURSE

AROUND the world there are thousands of fatal car accidents every day, but what are the chances of one vehicle being associated with *ten* accidents?

Hollywood legend James Dean, star of *Rebel Without A Cause*, had a love of racing sports cars. In the summer of 1955 he saw a silver grey Porsche Spyder on a Los Angeles forecourt and was instantly drawn to it. He bought the car and nicknamed it 'Little Bastard', which tragically turned out to be very apt.

Many of his actor friends did not share Dean's love of the car. Alec Guinness, Ursula Andress and Nick Adams, star of the television series *The Rebel*, all expressed an uneasiness when they were around the Little Bastard. George Barris, a car designer who had worked on Dean's other racers, also talked of a feeling of apprehension. Even the actor's uncle told Dean it gave him the creeps. He just shrugged it all off and joked, saying he was destined to die in a speeding car anyway. The film star did not realise he was speaking the literal truth.

He was due to race the car in Salinas on 1 October and was leaving Los Angeles to make the journey when the accident happened. With him was a Porsche mechanic, Rolf Wuetherich. Out on the open and apparently deserted highway Dean decided to open up the throttle to see what the car could do.

Racing over the brow of a hill he was confronted with a Ford Sedan which was turning left on to the road. With only a split second in which to make a decision, the driver, a student by the name of Donald Turnupseed, froze. Dean was travelling far to fast to brake and slammed head on into the Sedan. The actor was killed instantly, but amazingly his passenger and the other driver survived.

James Dean's premature death shocked the world, but the tragedy associated with the car was destined to continue. George Barris bought the wreck for parts, but, when it was being unloaded at his garage, it fell on a mechanic, breaking one of his legs. The engine and drive chain were sold to two doctors named Troy McHenry and William Eschrid. Once fitted with parts from the Little Bastard McHenry's car mysteriously went out of control on its first run and the doctor died. Eschrid survived with terrible injuries when his modified car rolled over while he was cornering.

Barris sold two undamaged tyres from the wreck to another sports car enthusiast. The young driver came back a few days later to tell Barris that *both* tyres had blown while he was out driving, nearly killing him as he fought to control the car.

Fans seeking souvenirs from the wreckage were injured too. One gashed his arm open while removing the steering wheel, and another was injured attempting to lift out a section of the blood-stained seat. George Barris had had enough. He turned the vehicle over to the California Highway Patrol for use in a road safety campaign. Even then the run of tragedy associated with the Porsche did not end.

At its third exhibition the garage used to store the vehicles burnt down, destroying the other cars, but leaving the Porsche untouched by fire. At the next show the Little Bastard fell off its stand, breaking an onlooker's hip. While it was being transported on a trailer, the driver lost control and died in the crash.

The accidents and injuries only ceased when the car mysteriously disappeared in 1960. It was used by the Florida Highway Patrol for an exhibition and was afterwards put on a truck for its return to Los Angeles. The truck arrived, but the car vanished, never to be seen again.

VEHICLE FOR DISASTER

A RED limousine that played its part in the start of World War I was later connected with a number of other tragedies.

The stage was set in the Bosnian city of Sarajevo – destined to become a theatre of war again during the 1990s. In 1914 Bosnia was in revolt against Austria. It was on 28 June that the Austrian Archduke Franz Ferdinand and his wife Sophie decided, against advice, to tour the city in an open-topped car. As their red limousine approached the corner of Rudolph Street, Franz

Ferdinand and Sophie were both shot dead by Gavrilo Princip, a student anarchist. The car survived the attack unscathed.

Some parapsychologists believe that strong emotional events – such as a murder – can become imprinted into the fabric of a house, for instance. The event then replays like a videotape recording, earning the house a reputation for being 'haunted'. Do curses work in a similar way? Was the horror of that moment imprinted into the bodywork of the red limousine so that all who owned it were tainted with the original violent act of death? Or was what followed simply a matter of 'chance'?

The car was bought by an Austrian General Potiorek. After his defeat in the Battle of Valjevo he became insane and died. Nine days after buying it, the next owner died in a crash. Then the Governor of Yugoslavia lost an arm in it. The car was then sold to a doctor who was crushed to death, followed by a Serbian farmer who died when he started it. A Swiss racing driver died when he was thrown from the vehicle over a wall. It was sold to a garage proprieter who, with four passengers, took it out for a run. They all died in a crash while overtaking another car. Finally the deadly vehicle ended up in a Vienna museum.

THE CURSE OF TUTANKHAMUN

ONE of the most infamous curses arose out of the opening of the tomb containing the Egyptian boy-king Tutankhamun. Egyptian tombs have a long reputation for placing curses on those who desecrate their holy burial chambers. One can view this as an example of the powers of an ancient and mysterious civilisation or as superstition designed to deter grave robbers from stealing the priceless treasures which were buried with the

Egyptian kings. Was it a consequence of the former that brought tragedy down on the heads of a team of archaeologists in 1920 or was it 'coincidence'?

Lord Carnarvon, who led the team to Egypt, was well aware of the supposed curse. Three months before he was ready to open the inner tomb a psychic called Cheiro warned him against it. When the wall was breached, Carnarvon entered the tomb with a frivolous challenge to the curse. At the very least this was tempting Fate. Arthur Weigall, one of the excavators, told him that, if he did not treat the place with more respect, he would not last six weeks. Weigall's warning was prophetic, but Carnarvon lasted more than six weeks – he survived seven, when a mosquito bite became infected and he died.

Lord Carnarvon was the first of many people associated with the excavation to die under unusual circumstances. Weigall himself was victim number twenty-one. The curse seemed to spread its tentacles beyond those directly associated with the dig.

In 1979 a television special called *The Curse of King Tut* was being filmed on location by Granada Television. It was to star Ian McShane, but something awful happened which was to delay filming. McShane was driving a vintage car when he felt a power take control of the vehicle and pull it towards a ravine. The actor jumped clear seconds before the vehicle plummeted to destruction. He escaped death, but one of his legs was broken in ten places.

When, in 1983, the television company put in a massive claim to Lloyds for the delay, the insurance people claimed it was due to negligence as the car brakes must have been faulty. The judge in the subsequent court case thought differently, however. Granada were eventually awarded a large undisclosed sum.

Another Egyptian curse was blamed for the death of explorer Walter Ingram in 1888. Four years earlier Ingram had brought to England the mummified hand of an ancient Egyptian princess. It had been clutching a gold plaque inscribed with the words: 'Whoever takes me away to a foreign country, will die a violent death, and his bones will never be found.' Ingram was hunting near Berbera, Somaliland, when a rogue elephant trampled him to death. His body was buried in a dried river bed. When an expedition was sent to recover his remains, they found that a flood had washed him away.

A GAME OF DEATH

THE bizarre similarities between actor Bruce Lee's death and that of his son occurred amid a string of macabre incidents.

Bruce Lee collapsed and died in 1973 at the age of thirty-two on the set of the film *Game of Death*. The character believes he is pursued by demons. In the film Bruce's character is shot when thugs replace a fake bullet with a real one. This image never left eight-year-old Brandon Lee, fearing it would be his fate too.

Twenty years after his father's death, on 31 March 1993 Brandon Lee was accidentally shot on the film set of *The Crow*. The shot fired by fellow actor, Michael Masse, severed his spine and he died a few hours later. It was discovered that the tip of a fake bullet had been left in the gun. Death took both father and son on the set of their fourth feature films.

The Crow was plagued with disaster. On 1 February, the first day of shooting, a carpenter was severely burned on his face, chest and arms when live power cables hit the crane in which he was working. On the same day the film unit's publicist was involved in a minor accident, and later that evening an equipment truck mysteriously caught fire.

A disgruntled sculptor working on the set suddenly went berserk and drove a car through the plaster shop. Then a construction worker slipped and drove a screwdriver through his hand. Just before Brandon's death mid-March storms destroyed the location sets.

Five weeks later saw the release of *The Dragon* – which featured Jason Scott Lee's depiction of Bruce Lee.

OUT OF THE FIRE INTO THE FRYING PAN

MARK and Diane Johnson of Neath, West Glamorgan, planned a dream holiday for themselves and their children in Australia. Their visit to Sydney, however, was cut short when devastating bush fires swept towards the city and they had to flee along with thousands of Australians. Determined to salvage something from the trip, they flew to the United States to visit relatives in Los Angeles. Little did they know that the worst was yet to come.

In the San Fernando Valley they began to relax and started to think about trips to the beach and Disney World. Then, at 4.30 in the morning, Mr Johnson was awoken by his wife screaming. The whole house was shaking. The family tried to escape, but the front door was blocked by the roof, which had caved in. They had to be dug out of the rubble by neighbours. It turned out they were at the epicentre of the Los Angeles earthquake. Safely back home once more in Scotland, Mr Johnson told reporters: 'We had been planning the trip for two years. I just wish we'd chosen different dates!'

CLINTON'S CURSE

HERE is a dire warning for all building developers who think a green field looks better when it's concreted over.

The medieval town of Kenilworth in Warwickshire seemed an ideal place to build a modern housing estate. In 1984 a planning application was submitted for eighty houses on land near Finham Brook. Subsequently the original applicant was killed in a hunting accident, the land changed hands three times as successive owners went bust, council officials were struck down by illness and both the chairman of the planning committee and the leader of the council lost their seats after agreeing to the application.

Local people who were against the development believe they have an ancient curse on their side made by the former owner of the land, one Geoffrey de Clinton. Henry I gave the Manor of Kenilworth to the knight around 1130; he then built a castle and a Benedictine abbey. De Clinton gave the people of Kenilworth the right to graze their livestock around the abbey and St Mary's Church. He left a warning that, if anyone 'should attempt to take away or diminish anything which I have granted to the aforesaid church, he shall incur the curse of his father and the anger of God.'

Avril Redman, whose family have lived in the town since Cromwell, said: 'The curse has passed into local folklore. The land has remained undeveloped for centuries. It's madness to build here.'

The land the developers were after formed the basin of the abbey's fishing lake, long since dried out – until recently. Despite drought in the area, the land has become waterlogged again. . . .

HOUSE OF HORROR

CERTAIN places develop a reputation for evil because of the way they look. Probably that was what was in the mind of Hammer Films when they chose Oakley Court as a location for Dracula and Frankenstein films. But the former Victorian country house, divided into flats, really did deserve its reputation.

The large Gothic building set on the banks of the River Thames at Bray had a number of deaths associated with it. In 1971 a man fell from a pleasure steamer and drowned opposite the house. A year later an old lady died in one of the flats and remained undiscovered for at least a week. But the worst series of tragedies involved the family of Mrs Penelope Gallereault, residents of Oakley Court.

Friends warned them of the unsavoury reputation of the place before they moved in. The horror began in the summer of 1972 when Mrs Gallereault saw hooded figures walking in the grounds. Then one morning she found a box on her doorstep. It contained the body of one of her cats – its neck broken. In December her two-year-old son, William, died. She was running him a bath and went to answer the telephone. On her return his body was floating in the water.

In August 1973 the couple lost another son – also by drowning. Two-year-old Edward was put inside his playpen in the grounds. Somehow he managed to escape and toddled down to the river, where he fell in. A month later Mr William Griffiths was sailing past Oakley Court, fixing the windscreen on his boat, when he fell in and also drowned – at the same spot as the other two deaths. Mr and Mrs Gallereault moved out after that.

The Rev. Sebastion Jones, curate of St Michael's Church, Bray, told reporters: 'Oakley Court is definitely spooky and I would not want to stay there myself. Evil can generate evil, and the grounds would be an ideal place to practise Black Magic.'

FIRE-STARTER

DURING 1973 Anthony Evans, a thirty-three-year-old security guard, complained of police harassment. An 'arson rampage' had terrorised the Forest Gate, Stratford and Canning Town areas of London with fifteen fires in two weeks. Mr Evans was found near six or eight of the fires, but claimed to be totally innocent. In September he told Charles Sandell of the *News of the World*: 'The police are harassing me because fires follow me around.'

The incidents involved two cars, two vans, a motorboat on a trailer, a pillarbox, a church, a school gymnasium and tuck shop. Then, on 28 August, three men died after someone apparently threw petrol into the Tudor Hotel, Stratford, setting it alight.

Mr Evans, who lived in Canning Town, vented his exasperation on Charles Sandell: 'Recently fires seem to happen wherever I go. The police seem to think I had something to do with starting them. It's ridiculous. I don't smoke. I don't carry matches. I think the police are trying to frame me for the fires!'

The first time it happened he was motoring along Upton Lane when he saw a church on fire. He stopped to call the Fire Service, but an appliance arrived as he looked for a telephone. Next he was in the vicinity of the expensive motorboat which burst into flames.

'Three of the fires have broken out near my home,' he said, 'It's just coincidence that I happened to be around at the time. But I've absolutely nothing to do with starting them.'

Scottish nanny Carol Compton was put on trial in Italy for attempted murder and arson in 1983. She had followed her Italian boyfriend there, who she had met in a Scottish hotel. But the relationship was over and Carol found work as a nanny. She worked for two families and a total of five fires erupted over three weeks before she was arrested.

The first fire occurred on 11 July 1982. She worked for the Ricci family at the time. While she was in the garden with the child and a maid, black smoke began pouring from the villa. The grandfather, who was inside, managed to escape, but £5,000 worth of damage resulted. Friends of the Riccis, the Morovers, offered the family and their nanny shelter. While they were there, a fire started in a waste bin. Then the grandfather had another lucky escape when it was discovered that the mattress he was lying on had begun smouldering. The finger of suspicion was pointed at Carol, even though there was no evidence. She was told to leave.

Within two weeks she was working for another family, looking after their three-year-old daughter Agnese. The Cecchinis took her to their holiday home on Elba. Carol did not get on with the little girl's grandparents. On 1 August Carol was relaxing in the sitting room when the grandfather's mattress was discovered on fire. One day later little Agnese's mattress started burning – while the child was sleeping on it. Fortunately she was rescued unharmed. After Carol was arrested, the mysterious fires which happened while she worked for the Riccis emerged.

There was never any evidence to directly link Carol Compton with any of the fires. Forensic tests ruled out accellerants, and experiments on similar mattresses failed to duplicate the pattern of burning on the originals. For the Italian authorities it was too much of a coincidence that Carol should have been in the vicinity of all the fires yet not responsible for setting them. In court she was acquitted of the attempted murder charge, but found guilty of arson and fire raising. She was released at the end of the trial because of the time already spent in prison.

Coincidence, or are people like Anthony Evans and Carol Compton capable of unconsciously causing things to burst into flame?

WITCHCRAFT

ALICE Hicks died under mysterious circumstances on 29 January 1978 in Youngstown, Ohio. Her neighbours believed her to be a witch. When detectives started investigating her death, they walked into a run of bad luck. It began when Detective Mike Gilboy removed a six-inch doll wrapped in ribbon from her house. Its head was turned backwards, there was a two-inch needle in its chest and a thorn pierced its back.

The day Detective Tony Cafaro put a report on Gilboy's desk, where the doll was kept, he slipped on some icy steps and broke his tail bone. Detective Joseph Fajack, who travelled to work with Gilboy, fell ill for the first time in twelve years. Other detectives connected to Mike Gilboy also began suffering health problems: Detective Clarence Green caught pneumonia, Lieutenant Don Malleske came down with flu – the first time in twenty years – and patrolman Sam DuBose, who took home some of Mrs Hicks's voodoo books to read, had all his top teeth removed. But it was Gilboy himself who suffered the most.

A week after taking the doll he almost choked to death on a pepper seed. The following day he pulled a shoulder muscle, and one month after that he had a double hernia and torn groin muscles. In March he caught Russian flu – but worse was to follow. He was pushed into an empty swimming pool, breaking his neck and back.

On 10 June Detective Steve Krispli removed the doll from Gilboy's desk to place it in an evidence locker. Four days later he was hospitalised with severe chest pains. This was the final straw. Lieutenant Sabatino burned the doll on 16 June.

THE WRATH OF MAUNALOA

AIRLINE vice-president Ralph Loffert from Buffalo, New York visited the volcanic Hawaiian island of Molokai with his wife and four children in the summer of 1977. While they were there, they collected lava rock from the Maunaloa volcano, despite warnings from the natives that this would anger the volcano goddess – Madame Pele.

Not long after they returned home Maunaloa erupted. This coincided with a run of bad luck for the Lofferts. Over a few months Todd, aged ten, developed appendicitis, had knee surgery and broke his wrist. Fourteen-year-old Mark sprained an ankle and broke his arm; Dan, aged eleven, caught an eye infection; and seven-year-old Rebecca lost two front teeth in a fall.

The Lofferts sent the stones to a friend in Hawaii, where they were returned to the volcano – but the bad luck continued. Mark hurt his knee, Rebecca lost three more teeth and Dan fractured his hand, while Todd dislocated an elbow and again fractured his wrist. At a loss what to do next, Mark confessed he had kept three of the rocks. When these were returned the series of disasters stopped.

STORMY WEATHER

SOMETIMES curses seem to revolve around an individual. For a beautiful Bulgarian woman named Martha Matikia, violent storms, death and three husbands were all rolled up together in a macabre series of coincidences.

It was during a storm in 1935 that she met her future husband, an American tourist called Randolph Eastman, when he sought shelter in her house. They were married within a week, but two months later he was struck dead by lightning. He left Martha £20,000. She bought her parents a new house with the money, and then married Charles Martaux. While on holiday in Spain, Charles was also struck by lightning.

She returned to Sofia and was treated for depression by a German doctor. When she had recovered, Martha went with him to Berlin and they were married. She left him upon discovering that he was a Nazi, but he followed her. Near the French border his car was struck by lightning, then he too was dead.

VOODOO CURSE

INDIVIDUALS who have been cursed as the result of voodoo rituals die, it is thought, because of the victim's *belief* in the power of the curse. It is a demonstration of mind over matter. Did a mother kill her son in this way or was it a tragic coincidence?

Finis P. Ernest of Oklahoma City was a fifty-three-year-old night club owner. In January 1960 he was admitted to the Veterans' Administration Hospital there suffering from asthma, but was soon discharged. Six months later, having been in and out of private hospitals as many times, he returned to the Veterans' Hospital, this time suffering fits and convulsions. Doctors, however, could find nothing organically wrong with him.

Having once again recovered, he left for his mother's house, but within two days he was stretchered back to the hospital, gasping for air and near death. Once again he recovered, although now the businessman was utterly depressed. He was allowed to visit his mother again and another relapse followed. By now his doctors were putting two and two together, and realised the two events were somehow connected. They let him leave the hospital only on condition he did not call round to see his mother. Finis P. Ernest was true to his word, but he suffered fatally anyway.

At about 6 pm on 23 August he had a telephone conversation with his mother. Just over half an hour later he was found gasping for breath. By 6.55 pm he was dead.

Curiosity got the better of Dr James P. Mathis and he decided to investigate. Dr Mathis discovered that upon the premature death of his father Finis had become 'man of the house' while still in his teens. This closer relationship with his mother resulted in her exerting a lot of influence over him. Before he was thirty Finis had married against the wishes of his mother twice, and in both cases had divorced. At thirty-one he and his mother opened a successful night club. Seven years later, with the approval of his mother, Finis married a schoolteacher called Josephine. All went well for fifteen years until, supported by his wife, he accepted an offer to sell the night club. Then the veiled threats began.

'Do this,' his furious mother warned, 'and something dire will happen to you!' Less than two days later he was struck down by asthma, but went ahead with the deal. Undefeated his mother continued with the threats. 'Something will strike you!' she yelled at him.

His health rapidly deteriorated and the hospitalisation began. The doctor's inability to protect him with pills and potions convinced Finis that mother's 'magic' was stronger. He had confided some of this to Dr Mathis, pointing out that so far his mother had proved to be infallible.

Josephine told Dr Mathis the last telephone call was to tell his mother that he planned to invest the money from the sale in a new venture – which would exclude her. She reminded him of the 'dire results' of his actions, and he was dead within the hour. Dr Mathis concluded that the case was a 'sophisticated version of a voodoo death'.

A SCOTTISH TRAGEDY

WILLIAM Shakespeare's play *Macbeth* has long had the reputation of being cursed. When one considers the long string of 'coincidences' associated with the play, one can see why. Many actors, including Peter O'Toole, consider it so cursed that they will not refer to it by name. According to actor-director Richard Huggett, the play was cursed from the very start when Shakespeare wrote genuine black magic incantations into the original text. It is perhaps not surprising that a play as powerful as *Macbeth*, concerned as it is with evil and the supernatural, should cast its black shadow on the outside world.

The 1937 production which played at the Old Vic was one of the most cursed. During rehearsals director Michel St Denis and leading lady Vera Lindsey were badly bruised in a car crash. The next day a dog belonging to Lilian Baylis, founder and director of the theatre, was run over and killed. At the dress rehearsal the sets would not fit, and Laurence Olivier, playing Macbeth for the first time, lost his voice. The opening night was postponed. Olivier escaped death when he was called on stage. Just as he left his seat in the wings a stage weight crashed down on it and broke it into pieces. Lilian Baylis had a heart attack and died on Friday, the night of the opening performance. During a sword fight a member of the audience was hit by a fragment from Olivier's weapon and died from a heart attack.

When the 1954 production went on tour, the company manager broke both legs in a car accident, an electrician received third-degree burns, there was an attempted suicide and two actresses had abortions.

In 1967 director Peter Hall started rehearsing *Macbeth* at Stratford-upon-Avon. He told the company that the curse did not exist. Then a theatre office clerk collapsed and died of a heart attack. Hall himself developed shingles, and for six weeks had to lie in a dark room. The production was postponed and, when it did eventually open that August, it was during a heatwave. The actors were wearing heavy plastic costumes and every night was torture.

The 1970 Liverpool Repertory Theatre production fared little better. In the second week of rehearsals the actor playing the lead was hit in the eye by a sword. After Lady Macbeth caught flu, it spread among the cast and five understudies took their places. Actor Jack Lynn was asked to take over the leading role, but he was still recovering from head injuries sustained in a production of the play in Chesterfield.

The list of tragedies associated with *Macbeth* could cover many pages. Are they really significant or is there a simple explanation? A play involving so many sword fights mostly in dim lighting is bound to encourage accidents on stage. As for the off-stage tragedies, has anyone done a comparison with other popular plays? Perhaps the power of *belief* is the key to the curse.

GONE TO THE MOON

WAS a curse unwittingly placed on a chemical factory by a would-be poet? When the NYPRO plant was first built in the mid 1960s at Flixborough, Lincolnshire, twenty-five men were sent to Holland for special training. Among them was a shift superintendent by the name of Fred Saxby. Fred celebrated the opening of the plant in 1966 by writing a poem entitled 'The Ballad of Big N', which was printed in the NYPRO Dutch newsletter. It contained the following verse:

> *So you can see that Nypro*
> *Sometime during June*
> *Could well be blown to pieces*
> *And be the first Plant on the Moon.*

On 1 June 1974 the Flixborough plant did indeed explode, causing considerable loss of life as well as damage to property and the environment.

SOURCES

Anderson, Ken, *Extraordinary Coincidences*, HarperCollins, 1993

Fortean Times, *Diary of a Mad Planet*, 1991

Fortean Times, *Gateways To Mystery*, 1993

Fortean Times, *Heaven's Reprimands*, 1994

Fortean Times, *Seeing Out The Seventies*, 1992

Fortean Times, *Yesterday's News Tomorrow*, 1992

Fairley, John, and Welfare, Simon, *Arthur C. Clarke's Chronicles of the Strange and Mysterious*, Collins, 1987

Gordon, Stuart, *The Book of Curses*, Headline, 1994

Jung, C.G., *Synchronicity*, Ark, 1985

Michell, John, and Rickard, Robert J.M., *Phenomena*, Thames & Hudson, 1983

Randles, Jenny, *Beyond Explanation*, Hale, 1985

Randles, Jenny, and Hough, Peter, *Death By Supernatural Causes?* Grafton, 1988

Randles, Jenny, and Hough, Peter, *Encyclopedia of the Unexplained*, O'Mara, 1995

Randles, Jenny, and Hough, Peter, *Scary Stories*, Futura, 1991

Ripley's Believe It Or Not! Strange Coincidences, Byron Press, 1990

INDEX